PREVENTING DROP-OUTS

By Richard N. Diggs

This guide will be helpful to those educators who feel
disturbed when any student drops out, regardless of how
incorrigible he or she was.

The challenge to retain and change our problem
students is one society can't ignore. We certainly can't
dismiss them with a "that's not my job" attitude and blame
parents who shouldn't be parents.

Someone must pick up the gauntlet. And it must be those
who stand before classrooms.

The alternative is building a prison the size of Nevada.

For information, call or write:

Progressive Publications
P.O. Box 640368
Beverly Hills, FL 34464-0368
(352) 527-8922

Street Address:
3617 N. Longpine Pt.
Beverly Hills, FL 34465

or fax your request to:
(352) 527-9004

Printed in the United States of America
ISBN 0-937157-14-7

Library of Congress Card Number
96-070272

Revised & reprinted, June 1999

DEDICATION

This book is dedicated to the memory of M. Robert Allen, Dean Emeritus, University of Miami, who passed away November 8th, 1995. As a friend and mentor, he will forever remain in my memory as the most extraordinary person I have every known.

CONTENTS

Preface

The older we get the more we worry about the world our grandchildren will have to live in and less about what we'll have to put up with for the rest of our lives. There is little doubt that they are going to have a much more difficult struggle than we had, particularly, if they don't stay in school long enough to gain a profession or at least some saleable skills.

That's why I have traveled extensively over the last twenty years spreading my gospel of retention.

The problem with any gospel, however, is that it is simply a composition of words unless someone does something with it. In other words, you can't taste a recipe by reading it.

Just as we need good cooks to bring recipes to a tasty conclusion, we need teachers who can best transfer knowledge.

Needless to say, I have seen my share of teachers who think reading a book out loud is doing enough to earn a paycheck, others that always beat their students to the parking lot.

Not until recently, however, did I get mad. Damn Mad!

Two years ago I began to put together a unique collection of posters which in my opinion would make students stop and think about their futures. Collectively, "they will create an incomparable campus attitude" I thought, and decided to find out if this were so.

I set an appointment with an English teacher I was

acquainted with who worked at a local Vo-Tech. As I had previously donated a number of books to him for his use, I figured he owed me a favor. I called him and set an appointment to meet.

On the designated day, I drove forty miles to his school. I arrived on time, but he wasn't there. I waited. He showed up about ten minutes later, but it was apparent he had forgotten about me. Instead of apologizing, however, he rudely said he couldn't talk to me now, as he had a meeting to go to which was a lot more important than meeting me.

I was irritated at my abrupt dismissal, but I told myself that the meeting must have been called on the spur of the moment, so what could he do?

When one of the other teachers told me that the meeting was scheduled "a few days ago", however, I wrote a letter to "Mr. Inconsiderate", telling him what I thought.

I received a phone call and an apology. My teacher did want to see the posters. Further, that he was really, "The salt of the earth" and I was really wrong in the assessment of him I had detailed in my letter. We set another appointment.

I delivered the posters, 60 laminated 12" x 18" practical messages of wisdom and guidance, ... designated primarily to keep students in school.

He will read them, he will see to it his associates read them, he will talk to the administrators at his school about them. "Come back in 3 weeks and you'll see!"

Three weeks later I returned. Not only were the numbered posters in complete disarray, but it became obvious "Mr.

Wonderful" had never even read them as he asked for advice on the retention of his students which, ironically, was very thoroughly spelled out in the content of the posters.

He then told me how he now was doing a great job with the 9 students who remained in his class out of the initial 21 he had started with. "It really was a blessing though", he said, "because the 12 who left never wanted to learn anyway."

This man serves today as a sad example of the thousands of teachers, many protected by tenure, who should not be allowed to stand in front of a classroom.

And that is why I find myself back at a keyboard.

Not that I can do much about ridding our system of all the teachers who should not be allowed to use that designation, but that I might be able to provide a few fresh ideas to those who proudly serve with caring hearts, ... who do feel bad when any classroom seat is suddenly unoccupied.

All young students must believe they can, and will, ... succeed!

To The Young

The great were once as you.
They whom men magnify to-day
Once groped and blundered on life's way,
Were fearful of themselves, and thought
By magic was men's greatness wrought.
They feared to try what they could do;
Yet Fame hath crowned with her success
the selfsame gifts that you possess.

The great were young as you,
Dreaming the very dreams you hold,
Longing yet fearing to be bold,
Doubting that they themselves possessed
The strength and skill for every test,
Uncertain of the truths they knew,
Not sure that they could stand to fate
With all the courage of the great.

Then came a day when they
Their first bold venture made,
Scorning to cry for aid.
They dared to stand to fight alone,
Took up the gauntlet life had thrown,
Charged full-front to the fray,
Mastered their fear of self, and then
Learned that our great men are but men.

Oh, Youth, go forth and do!
You, too, to fame may rise;
You can be strong and wise.
Stand up to life and play the man -
You can if you'll but think you can;
The great were once as you.
You envy them their proud success?
'Twas won with gifts that you possess.

Edgar A. Guest

Progressive Publications 1996.

To receive a poster catalog call (352) 382-1452   No. 021

CHAPTER 1

WHY IT IS NOW MORE IMPORTANT TO KEEP STUDENTS IN SCHOOL THAN IT EVER HAS BEEN BEFORE !

A few years into the next century it is forecast that Medicare will go broke. Everyone believes those in power will never allow this to happen, however, so why worry. Certainly, government won't stand idly by as ever increasing numbers of elderly Americans live longer and longer.

Probably not, but who will pay the bill? Obviously, those who are working, paying taxes, and yet living at a standard that could be labeled "inadequate."

The world of the future won't be short on jobs but most definitely will be short on jobs which pay a decent wage. The chasm between the "haves" and the "have nots" will continue to grow. Two parents working full time at minimum wage jobs will still fall below the poverty line.

Hasn't this always been so? What makes things different now? Because each of us must necessarily compete with the workers of the world, not just those in our town or State or Country.

How does U.S. Education compare with our global competitors? Not very well. As a matter of fact American students rank near the bottom in all international scholastic competitions.

What Every Student Should Know About Our National Debt

- The National Debt is the total amount of money which has been borrowed by the U.S. Government to pay the country's bills. The amount of this debt is now about 4 trillion dollars, or about $13,000 for every man, woman and child in the United States.

- At the present time our country is still spending far more each day than we are collecting in taxes and fees, consequently our National Debt continues to grow.

- Of all the money the Government takes in taxes and fees we now must use over $22.00 out of every $100.00 collected to pay the interest on our debt.

- Unless we as a nation begin to live with a balanced budget, that is, the amount we take in is the only amount we spend, then the percentage our government must pay out in interest will continue to increase.

- Who actually must pay this debt? You and your children and their children. How? Simply by not receiving benefits from the government in ratio to the amount paid in. Simply put, starting next year you will pay $100.00 in taxes and get $75.00 back in the form of federal benefits like paved roads, welfare payments, new Federal prisons, etc.

- In reality, is it possible to balance our budget? Yes, but like business, there are only two reasonable ways of accomplishing this, 1) Bringing in more money (usually raising taxes) or 2) Cutting expenses.

- Under "Cutting Expenses" we could make substantial gains if we had more of our citizens contributing to the "Kitty" and less people drawing out of the "Pot."

- Our students can assist in the challenge of balancing our National Budget and reducing our National Debt by numerous methods.
  Among Them:
  A) Stay in school, learn, graduate, go on to specialized education, graduate, go to work, pay taxes.
  B) Do your best to keep all your classmates from dropping out. In our major cities approximately 50% of all inner-city students drop out of High School. The vast majority subsequently are the cause of an expense society must pay, either as welfare recipients or prisoners.

Progressive Publications © Copyright 1996.
To receive a poster catalog call (352) 382-1452   No. 057

To further complicate the picture, studies indicate that the average U.S. employee works at a pace equal to 40% of his or her productive capability.

Why? Well, certainly one reason could be that only one in four U.S. workers say they like their jobs.

There is little doubt that each of us is far more efficient when we are working on projects we like doing, so it makes sense to design a system of education which, from the early grades, pays attention to the aptitudes and desires of each individual child.

A few years ago, we heard screams from Washington because someone learned how pathetic the average U.S. student measured up in math. So they advocated that everyone should know more math. To me this is downright stupid. Let those students who desire careers which need math to take more math. Leave the others to follow their own career paths to learn whatever is necessary to fulfill their career and employment objectives.

If I were king, I would advocate that only one subject be mandated from pre-kindergarten on up, the ability to read, whether you like to read or not.

Let's face it! Advancing in any career depends on one's ability to read. Even if we were to go so far as having this be the only subject offered in our early grades, let it be so. Wouldn't this restrict our children's ability to draw within the lines? Perhaps, but wouldn't it be nice to live in a country where any third grader can read fluently and with comprehension?

If we look at our prison population today, you'll find that about 75% cannot read at an eighth grade level and 50%

PRESS ON

NOTHING IN THE WORLD CAN TAKE THE PLACE OF PERSISTENCE. TALENT WILL NOT; NOTHING IS MORE COMMON THAN UNSUCCESSFUL MEN WITH TALENT. GENIUS WILL NOT; UNREWARDED GENIUS IS ALMOST A PROVERB. EDUCATION ALONE WILL NOT; THE WORLD IS FULL OF EDUCATED DERELICTS. PERSISTENCE AND DETERMINATION ALONE ARE OMNIPOTENT.

can be considered functionally illiterate. Is it any wonder that when released, over 40% will find their way back behind bars. They simply can't compete for today's better paying jobs and their choices for survival will, of course, include illegal activities.

From this scenario, at least two conclusions can be drawn: One, prisoners must be able to read as a condition of release and two, they must submit a plan indicating how they intend to support themselves when they are released.

To prevent this procedure from reoccurring twenty years down the road, however, we can start now to see to it that illiteracy is eliminated for all Americans by the time they reach eight years of age.

It sure will be a lot cheaper than paying the $25,000 per prisoner per year price tag for an ever increasing number of those who aren't prepared to be contributing members of society.

If we are to recreate an America which can live with a balanced budget, we must eliminate every expense we can which is now spent for those who are not contributing to the National kitty ...

How? There is only one way, ... a better system of education which allows each student to explore the opportunities which can best serve his or her desires.

In other words, we must build a work force which is comprised of citizens who enjoy going to work each day, ... as they are employed in endeavors which they themselves have chosen.

This book deals with keeping students in school as long as it takes for them to become happily employed productive citizens.

God help us if this is not possible.

SEE IT THROUGH

When you're up against a trouble,
   Meet it squarely, face to face;
Lift your chin and set your shoulders,
   Plant your feet and take a brace.
When it's vain to try to dodge it,
   Do the best that you can do;
You may fail, but you may conquer,
   See it through!

Black may be the clouds about you
   And your future may seem grim,
But don't let your nerve desert you;
   Keep yourself in fighting trim.
If the worse is bound to happen,
   Spite of all that you can do,
Running from it will not save you,
   See it through!

Even hope may seem but futile,
   When with troubles you're beset,
But remember you are facing
   Just what other men have met.
You may fail, but fall still fighting;
   Don't give up, whate'er you do:
Eyes front, head high to the finish.
   See it through!

Edgar A. Guest

Progressive Publications 1996.

To receive a poster catalog call (352) 382-1452   No. 028

CHAPTER 2

UNDERSTANDING WHY STUDENTS DROP OUT

First we should point out that as this book goes to print about 40 million adult Americans over the age of 25 do not have a high school education.

Our attrition rate has not changed in decades. At least 25% of all U.S. High School students drop out, and in our major cities the figure continues to remain around 50%.

With fewer and fewer jobs each year being available for the unskilled, it is frightening to think what society will do with the enormous numbers who aren't educationally prepared to make a self-sustaining wage.

Back in the late sixties, I performed a survey in the city of Detroit. Of every 100 kids who started High School half dropped out. Of those who graduated, many of whom couldn't read their diplomas, half went on to some type of post-secondary education. Of these, half dropped out. Final analysis: 12 1/2% of those who started High School in the City of Detroit ultimately gained some saleable skills at the post-secondary level which would allow them to be employable at above average wages.

The question then, as it is now, : What are we going to do with the other 87 1/2 % ?

And let us not think that Detroit is different than any other major city. If we were to analyze the statistics in any big city, they would be very much the same.

It is obvious we must do everything we can at every level of education, public and private, to keep students in school.

In the mid-seventies I decided to find out why students dropped out and in preparation of a book on the subject, I solicited the help of school administrators from coast to coast. Their contributions were significant. Hundreds of letters were received, each detailing the feelings and assumptions of those at their institutions. Few, however, related factual responses from those who had dropped out. It appeared as if after students were discovered missing, there was no need to find out why they weren't there. "Out of sight, out of mind." "If they want to come back, let them reapply." Sad!

As simple as it may seem, however, one thing became very clear. Students drop out because they don't want to be there. Something else in their lives is more important than being in school.

An old adage came to mind, "Nobody ever does anything they don't want to do, considering the alternatives they have."

Sure we don't like taking out the garbage, but we do so because the alternative is having a stench in the kitchen and having insects crawling all over everything.

You go to the ballet when you would rather be at the fights because of a trade off with the spouse which makes your life a little more tension free. Your decision is made in your own best interests even though you don't share your husband's devotion to dancers who like to perform on their toes.

Understanding this, we then realized that the answer to the drop-out problem was simply "Making Students want to be there!"

If a student would rather be attending your school than doing anything else, then there obviously would be no reason for him or her to drop out. Right? Absolutely!

All we have to do then is to motivate students to stick around, to like coming to school, to like working harder, to like the other students, to like the subjects they are studying, to like the teachers, etc., in short, to like their lives while attending your school.

Can this be done. Certainly! All we need is a plan.

We certainly can't continue to operate our schools as we have been. - We must learn from the mistakes of the past and try the things that haven't been done before.

The Things That Haven't Been Done Before

The things that haven't been done before,
  Those are the things to try;
Columbus dreamed of an unknown shore
  At the rim of the far-flung sky,
And his heart was bold and his faith was strong
  As he ventured in dangers new,
And he paid no heed to the jeering throng
  Or the fears of the doubting crew.

The many will follow the beaten track
  With guideposts on the way,
They live and have lived for ages back
  With a chart for every day.
Someone has told them it's safe to go
  On the road he has traveled o'er,
And all that they ever strive to know
  Are the things that were known before.

A few strike out, without map or chart,
  Where never a man has been,
From the beaten paths they draw apart
  To see what no man has seen.
There are deeds they hunger alone to do;
  Though battered and bruised and sore,
They blaze the path for the many, who
  Do nothing not done before.

The things that haven't been done before
  Are the tasks worth while to-day;
Are you one of the flock that follows, or
  Are you one that shall lead the way?
Are you one of the timid souls that quail
  At the jeers of a doubting crew,
Or dare you, whether you win or fail,
  Strike out for a goal that's new?

Edgar A. Guest

Progressive Publications 1996.

In Every Adversity
There Is The
Equivalent
Of An Equal
Or Greater Benefit

Look For It!

The Six Mistakes of Man

1. The delusion that personal gain is made by crushing others.

2. The tendency to worry about things that cannot be changed or corrected.

3. Insisting that a thing is impossible because we cannot accomplish it.

4. Refusing to set aside trivial preferences.

5. Neglecting development and refinement of the mind, and not acquiring the habit of reading and studying.

6. Attempting to compel others to believe and live as we do.

The Roman philosopher and statesman, Cicero, wrote this some 2000 years ago.

CHAPTER 3

AN INTRODUCTION TO THE
MOTIVATING FACTORS OF MANKIND

To organize our plan we are going to look at what makes any of us do anything, ... *THE MOTIVATING FACTORS OF MANKIND*, four categories which cover the breadth of all human desire.

Once you know them, you will possess the knowledge to influence anyone. They are also the way any of us can break the preoccupation of those who don't appear to be listening to us.

Remember them: **ROMANCE, RECOGNITION, MONEY AND WHAT IT WILL BUY,** AND **SELF PRESERVATION.**

ROMANCE: Yes it does mean love and kisses as you might expect, but then so much more as this category includes anything we like to do such as, reading, sailing, traveling, watching TV, playing a sport, having a hobby, an avocation, a vocation, ... and on and on. There are many ways we can romance students so they will stay in school. In ensuing chapters we will show you how this can be done.

RECOGNITION: From birth we cry for attention, then graduate to all kinds of ploys and devices as we grow older, to say to the world, "Here I am." In high school it may be the label on a pair of jeans or having gym shoes "like Mike's."

It could also be the colors or the clothes that indicate gang membership, or the car we drive, or the jewelry we wear, or even the type of mustard we keep in our glove box. It is our desire to be recognized either for good or evil or just being somebody. Many students go through their entire school years known only by derogatory nicknames or obscure references such as "Hey you!" We are going to use recognition to keep students in school. We will show you very specifically how this can be done.

MONEY & WHAT IT WILL BUY: Since the advent of the industrial revolution, owning and using the new products which seem to be introduced daily have taken precedence over honing personal relationships. Greed seems to be reaching epidemic proportions unheard of just 100 years ago. For our purposes, however, it may help us keep students in school.

SELF-PRESERVATION: To remain alive is the obvious motivation in this category, but it also entails being in good physical and emotional health. If someone were to step out of a dark alley with a gun in his hand and say, "Stick 'em up", there is little doubt that most of us would be motivated to react. Fear makes us respond, but for our purposes the opposite is also true, so our motivating tools will also include "the absence of fear."

In the following Chapters we will list tried and true suggestions in each of the aforementioned categories which you can use at your school to keep students in school.

As you read, consider other ideas which you can add to your own plan to prevent attrition.

CHAPTER 4

THE ATTITUDE WHICH ALL EFFECTIVE EDUCATORS MUST ASSUME

If we are to diminish the attrition rate in this country all administrators and teachers must understand that we can't justify the loss of any student at any level with a "good riddance" sigh of relief.

As much as some kids are a pain in the neck (or some other part of the anatomy) we can't just pass them on to somebody else to handle knowing full-well they don't deserve to advance. Neither can we conceive a plot to rally support for the expulsion of a "headache" regardless of how much better it would make our lives.

At every level of our system, we must accept the challenge of straightening out the minds of children who belong to parents who never could have qualified to be mothers or fathers were it necessary to be tested for these positions.

At the elementary level we must sow dreams, helping each child to use his or her "theatre of the mind".

Although a person may change his or her career objectives many times throughout his or her lifetime, when we have one we are concentrating on we are at that time, ... better, more productive students.

Really! This actually applies to young children? Yes!

ATTITUDE

Attitude is our disposition, our thoughts, our feelings, our opinions. They can be bad or good, weak or powerful, negative or positive. If negative they will stymie all progress, all achievement, all chance of living happily ever after. If positive they become more important than being attractive, coming from money or knowing people in high places. Positive attitudes will win more games, win more contests, win more races than ever won by those who depend on talent alone. Those with positive attitudes will realize that if in fact no one loves them, it could be the result of not being lovable. They will see beauty in an ugly child, see glasses half full rather than half empty, see days partly sunny rather than partly cloudy, see benefits in all adversity. It is these optimists, who can visualize desirable tomorrows, who will have the strength to say no to drugs, no to drinking excessively, no to smoking, no to irresponsible sex.

Knowing our attitudes will create certain and predictable futures, we must choose paths which eliminate all reference to failure and concentrate forever on "I must," "I can," "I will." When we take charge of our attitudes, we cannot help but progress and succeed and share and benefit from reactions to our deeds. Learning, winning, happiness, friendships, and good fortune will inevitably come our way.

Billy Rodgers

Attitude Is Everything!

Progressive Publications 1996.

Assist each child to have a serious response to the question, "And what are you going to be when you grow up?" and you'll have a better student and one who will respond very favorably to praise and recognition.

Someone once said, "no child starts out dreaming about being a drug dealer". Well I'm not so sure of this if the only examples of elaborate living in some neighborhoods is that shown by those peddling "white powder that makes you feel good."

Teachers must assume the obligation of fashioning legitimate dreams, and further these with field trips, and an abundance of encouraging words.

Middle School and High School teachers must pick up the gauntlet by assisting all students to visualize their career and employment objectives. Then, thereafter, sharing these dreams and continually offering suggestions regarding the paths one might better choose.

That's the job of the Guidance Counselor! Nonsense! It is a role all of us must assume.

And speaking of "what must be done" let's also tackle the subject of morality.

In 1993, Michael Sovern resigned as president of Columbia University. A reporter asked him if there were any task he had left incomplete.

"Yes", he replied. "It sounds complacent, but there is really only one, the lack of instruction in ethics." He pointed out that although professional schools, such as Law, Medicine, and Business Administration, offer some pretty good programs in professional ethics, the average undergraduate receives no such training.

Why? Because most educators, from grammar school through college, are afraid to touch the subjects. Topics such as these are usually addressed by parents or members of religious organizations. The result is that in this country, young people who need moral and ethical training more than ever are getting less than ever.

Morals and ethics are not religion. They are logical, sensible principles of good conduct that we need to maintain a peaceful, productive society.

Please don't pass off the responsibility of teaching these principles to someone else. Just don't start quoting scripture. Stick to common sense anecdotes which make it plain that moral conduct is necessary if a society is to be sustained.

When Thomas Jefferson created the state-run University of Virginia, he insisted that it have no religious affiliation. Yet he insisted that "moral philosophy" be a required course of study.

Aside from setting an example, consider what you might do to teach good moral conduct. Certainly, motivating students by showing them how ethical practices are the surest way to success and happiness can be explored.

Now, let's get back to assisting students to create career and employment goals.

When we speak of motivating factors, a gift to someone which includes two of the four factors is a gift that is sure to be appreciated. A gift which includes three factors would be fantastic. And a gift that includes all four factors would be simply awesome!

Is there such a thing as a four-factor gift?

Yes, there is, but only one that we know of. It is called "AN IDEAL JOB."

That's the job that we love going to each day (Romance), that affords us praise from encouraging, appreciative bosses, (Recognition), that provides us with a good wage (Money), that allows us to live fear-free in a healthy, crime-free neighborhood (Self Preservation).

When you help anyone foresee themselves in their "Ideal Job" you are providing the greatest service any teacher can provide. And you will long be remembered as being "the one person who changed my life."

Now if the Elementary teachers, the Middle School teachers and the High School teachers did their jobs, the Post-Secondary educators must simply keep their students focused on their specific career and employment objectives and refuse to allow any of them to give up.

That's the attitude we all must have. "I must accept the responsibility of seeing to it that no student I know of drops out of school."

Now let's use these factors to make sure no student here-after drops out.

We will get back to the subject of "Getting Ideal Jobs" later in Chapters 9 and 10.

Creed for Optimists

Be so strong that nothing can disturb your peace of mind. Talk health, happiness, and prosperity to every person you meet. Make all your friends feel there is something in them. Look at the sunny side of everything. Think only of the best, work only for the best, and expect only the best. Be as enthusiastic about the success of others as you are about your own. Forget the mistakes of the past and press on to the greater achievements of the future. Give everyone a smile. Spend so much time improving yourself that you have no time left to criticize others. Be too big for worry and too noble for anger.

Christian D. Larsen

Progressive Publications 1996.

CHAPTER 5

USING THE ROMANCE FACTOR TO INFLUENCE STUDENTS

The following ideas are presented in no particular order and may or may not apply to you, your school, or your environment. For the most part they are simply common sense thoughts which have been proven to be effective. Take them and use them.

1. *Physical Appearance*

How does your school look? How does your class room look? Often, after years of coming to work, we lose sight of what the place looks like. Tomorrow, try to view your campus and your immediate working area as if you are seeing it for the first time.

Ask yourself if it is appealing?, colorful?, warm?, exciting?, a place a young person would like to come?

We can't very well keep a student in school if we can't get him or her there in the first place. At the post-secondary level students have a choice. Liking what they see may easily be the factor which moves them to enroll.

Very often, the decor in our classrooms and school hallways is strikingly similar to what you would see in our correctional institutions. It's bad enough to have many of our kids thinking of schools as prisons without confirming their opinions by using decorating schemes which might be labeled, "Early Alcatraz" or "Attica Avocado."

If your inspection reveals the belief that improvements could help make your place more appealing without being borax, too bold, or offensive to some, ... get going. Consider: wallpaper, paint, flags, plants, pictures, posters, signs, trim, statues, collages, models, costumes, bumper stickers, maps, ... whatever.

Eliminate: dirt, cobwebs, obsolete equipment, old books, broken stuff, hand-written signs, tape holding nothing, graffiti, cords which are a safety hazard, closet clutter, and anything which is obviously passé.

Your challenge is to get the first time viewer to say "Wow!" rather than "Ugh!"

2. **If you don't have a TV monitor elevated in each classroom do whatever you can to get them there as soon as possible.**

Prospective students taking the campus tour will be impressed if they are greeted in each room by an old familiar friend, the TV set. To most students a monitor suggests an easier way to learn. And this may be a very accurate assumption if you use them.

Adding to your own library of tapes is also a fine method of romancing your students. You can even make tapes of yourself to use when for some reason neither you or a substitute is available.

Tapes are also an excellent help for those students who have been absent and need help to catch up with the class. As most homes now have a VCR, all kinds of tutoring tapes can now be used to romance and encourage your students.

There is absolutely no doubt that students who get behind for whatever reason are subject to dropping out.

3. Once enrolled, romance those prospective students so they don't change their minds about starting school.

Certainly, proprietary school people are more conscious of the term "no-show" than those in public schools because the private sector suffers an immediate financial loss when a student fails to show up for class.

Chances are we would have far fewer drop-outs in this country at all levels if every teacher received a little less in their paychecks every time a student failed to start their class or subsequently dropped out.

Here are a few suggestions to romance students after they enroll so they will not renege on their intention to start school.

A) Have your enrollment representatives record all the applicant's interests, hobbies, avocations, vocations, etc. as divulged in the interview process. This information should be included in the student's permanent file to be used later. When a student needs to be motivated, teachers, counselors, and administrators will find this data to be helpful.

B) Encourage your enrollment personnel to watch for articles in newspapers and magazines which correspond with the interests of enrollees who have some time to go before they start school. Then send the articles to the potential students with a note like the following: "When I saw this article on Ham Radio, I thought of you." "Thought you might find it of interest!" "Look forward to seeing you soon." "Jim Davis."

C) Send a warm letter to all parents and personal references of the prospective student, signed by the Administrative head of the school. Tell them that you intend to offer an education second to none but it could be of greater benefit to the student if they encouraged the student to be the best they can be.

D) If you are a post-secondary education administrator, direct employees to send similar letters to the counselors at the High School from which each prospect came. Romance them by assuring them you will be providing each student with a sound education as well as ongoing placement training. Send copies of your school news-paper with the letter.

E) Send notices along with photos of new enrollees to local newspapers. Write the article for the newspaper announcing the student's enrollment so it is simple for the editor to send it on for typesetting. In the article be sure you mention the High School the enrollee came from and the career path she or he has chosen. In addition to romancing these enrollees you will be using a little psychology which will make it more difficult for them to change their minds about attending.

    NOTE: It will serve you well to initiate a procedure whereby four photos of the enrollee are taken at the time of enrollment. One is to be affixed to the outside of the Student File. The second used to notify newspapers as indicated above. The third used internally on bulletin boards and for articles in the School Newspaper, and the fourth used to send to newspapers with an announcement of the student's graduation.

4. *Aptitudes are actually romance factors. Make sure you enroll no students who don't have an aptitude for the subject matter.*

Back in the early fifties, TV was just being introduced. It prompted a social phenomenon. As soon as a set was purchased, the children in the family became instantly popular. Kid crowds formed daily at every house with an aerial. It was a real status symbol but it was also a headache for these mothers. They had to become discerning policemen overnight, trying to decide who was a close enough friend to enter and who wasn't.

It didn't take a genius to figure out that there was going to be a lot of money made in everything associated with TV. A friend of mine promptly enrolled in an expensive TV Repair course which a local school had just initiated. He had absolutely no aptitude for electronics, in fact he admitted he hated it, but said the money he was going to make would make it worthwhile.

Then one day he read some wise advice that Confucius said a few thousand years ago: .... "Choose a job you love and you'll never have to work a day in your life." It made him think again. He asked himself what was more important, being happily employed at an average wage or working at a job he hated just to make a few more dollars? He naturally concluded he would rather be happily employed and promptly dropped out of school.

Making sure your applicants possess the right reasons for taking a class or a course is important. Find out if they belong. It is also important to determine if they have the educational prerequisites to take a class or a course before they waste their money. Setting goals is important for all of us, as we will discuss in depth later, but unless the goals are realistically obtainable, they should be reconsidered. Whether enrolling for a class or a course, turn down every applicant who doesn't have a reasonable chance to succeed.

Some years ago, I owned an Auto & Diesel Mechanic School in Michigan. We were fussy about who we admitted because we knew that enrolling any warm body was simply inviting drop-outs in addition to lowering the quality of the instruction. Our diploma was valuable and our reputation was well documented. We were probably the first school in Michigan to turn down students referred to us by government agencies like Rehabilitation.

Other school owners called me crazy, but it paid off. After their initial shock, Rehabilitation counselors sent more applicants because they knew we would carefully evaluate every applicant's chances for success.

Now we also had a considerable number of women who applied and we accepted quite a few. But we turned down more than we accepted as their reasons for wanting to take the course very often indicated they had no desire to work in this field. "The boy I am interested in is a mechanic and I just know if I can talk car talk I can get him to like me."

Usually, drawing a visual picture of "oil and grease under every finger nail" and "all kinds of fluids dripping in your face while you lay on your back under an engine in the middle of winter" helped most of these young girls to change their minds.

Bottom line: If you make sure your applicants can benefit from the class or course they are applying for, you'll have far fewer drop-outs. If a requirement exists, which in your opinion is not necessary to reach the objective, do your best to change the prerequisites.

5. **Before a school can create and maintain an enviable image in a community, every member of the staff and faculty must sincerely care about student success.**

Nobody can foster the attitude, "that's not my job."

Those hiring at the school must learn how to hire. So very often a new employee is added to the payroll in haste because a vacancy exists that "has to be filled immediately." Nonsense! Don't accept anyone until you are convinced they fit into your "family" atmosphere.

It only takes one incorrigible faculty member to turn the entire morale of a school upside down. Don't allow this to happen.

A) Study every book in the library relevant to hiring.

B) Consult hiring specialists. There are many excellent pre-employment psychological tests on the market today which will help you clone some of your best faculty members. Keep in mind that personality characteristics are often far more important factors in hiring compatible co-workers than is a long list of degrees.

C) When hiring faculty members do so on a 45 day trial basis if at all possible.

When hiring faculty members, also let them know that their students will be asked to grade them on a percentile basis from time to time. This is a procedure often used in proprietary schools to determine both customer satisfaction and instructor competence. If this is allowed where you work, create a *Student Critique* and use it.

At schools I owned, every time the faculty as a whole received a collective grade from the student body of 95% or above, the entire faculty and their spouses were treated to a dinner at a fine local restaurant. The student critique survey became an event the faculty looked forward to rather than a day they resented.

If you can use this at your school, try it. You'll find it to be a helpful tool to bring your "family members" a little closer together.

D) Never hire anyone without a thorough background check.

Remember, .. the greatest con men in the world are also the most likeable. Take the time to do it right.

Your primary responsibility as an administrator is to find teachers who love to teach.

6. **Make sure all new students leave after the first day of class with very favorable opinions of the school, the teachers and the other students.**

The first day of class is extremely important as more drop-outs occur early in programs than as time goes by. Here are a few suggestions to use to romance your new students:

A) Set up a Big Brother-Little Brother and Big Sister-Little Sister arrangement with all students. Your older students are paired off with your new students to show them around and make them feel at home.

   This can be a voluntary program if you so wish.

B) Hold a comprehensive Orientation the first day of class, if not before. At the orientation, have each member of your faculty introduce themselves, tell what they do, say what hours they are available for consultation, and then state "if I can ever help you with anything, please come and see me!"

   If all your faculty members are sincere when providing their statements, a new student can't help but feel his or her choice in schools was a wise one.

C) Consider forming *Study Groups* comprised of 5 to 7 students with the same career objectives. A monitor subsequently challenges the members of each group with the responsibility of seeing to it no member of that group drops out. Group projects center around progressive steps members can take to find better than average jobs. All members pledge to help other members with solutions to both school related and personal problems.

D) Have a *Newcomer's Picnic* or *Newcomer's Party* that first day. The school foots the bill. Introduce games which are designed to encourage mixing and

FRIENDS

It is said that the sum of our existence is responding to the needs of just one person. Take it upon yourself to reach further, ... and you will gain more!

What is a friend? ... An acquaintance who helps, who doesn't just advise, ... who flatters you at those times when you are experiencing emotional fatigue, ... who deals in deeds, not intentions, ... who very often provides unselfish favors without thoughts of reciprocation, ... who volunteers to carry more than the stool when the piano needs moving, ... who understands that loving is sharing both the good and the bad, ... who is the drying towel which absorbs flowing tears, ... who stands patiently by when you are behaving at your ugly worst, ... who answers the door with you when trouble comes calling, ... who takes pleasure in having the last word only when it is an apology, ... who knows how to say nothing ... and when.

You will recognize a friendship whenever you are at ease living, laughing and loving, for it is then you will realize that friends multiply joy and divide sorrow.

But friendships just don't happen, ... they are gifts we give ourselves.

Choose today to cultivate those you meet, for the rewards are plentiful and no law dictates that you cannot have more than one.

Think about it! No possession on this planet, regardless of dollar cost, is as valuable as having another human being you can truly call ..... your friend!

It could easily be that the wealthiest one among us ..... doesn't have a dime!

James Bradford

To receive a poster catalog call (352) 382-1452   No. 091

meeting others.

NO STUDENT SHOULD LEAVE CAMPUS THAT
FIRST DAY WITHOUT FEELING THAT THEY
HAVE MADE SOME NEW AND PROMISING
FRIENDSHIPS.

7. Have a student lounge where food and snacks can be purchased for less than the prices charged at local stores.

Not only will you be romancing many students who
will appreciate the fact they can save money, but
you will be keeping students on campus and this is
important.

Anytime students gather off campus during school
hours there is a temptation to go elsewhere on some
whim to do something crazy or irresponsible.

8. Have annual trips planned. One for everyone, others for student groups with common interests.

There is little doubt that extra-curricular activities will
keep students coming to school. Often, however,
their focus becomes almost exclusively sports, the
choir, the school play, etc. Studies become
secondary.

Trips can be used as incentives, rewarding those
who qualify as the result of their performance in
class.

A school WEEKEND CRUISE can be planned. All
students in good standing will be eligible to
attend.

SMILE

A smile costs nothing, but it creates much.

It happens in a flash, and the memory of it may last forever.

It enriches those who receive it without impoverishing those who give it.

None are so rich that they can get along without it, and none so poor that they cannot be richer for its benefits.

It creates happiness in the home, fosters goodwill in a business, and is the countersign of friends.

It is rest to the weary, daylight to the discouraged, sunshine to the sad, and nature's best antidote for trouble.

Yet it cannot be begged, bought, borrowed, or stolen, for it is something that is worth nothing to anyone until it is given away.

In the course of the day, some of your acquaintances may be too tired to give you a smile. Give them one of yours.

Nobody needs a smile so much as those who have none left to give.

Progressive Publications 1996.

Trips for small groups, clubs, teams can also be planned to correspond with the common interests of the participants.

Auto Mechanic students can be scheduled to go to the Indianapolis 500.

Computer students can be the guests of a Las Vegas casino where they will be shown how the computer plays a role in all aspects of management.

Even trips to Europe can be planned years in advance so that each student can earn an accumulation of "school dollars" for school service, exemplary attendance, tutoring those who need help, fund raising for school needs, academic improvement, etc.

Each *school dollar* in an account will reduce the fare a student will have to pay for *The Great Senior Trip.*

Students motivated by the desire to attend future events will seldom drop out.

9. *Motivate students to join in an organized effort to help others.*

Your school will always benefit when a group of your students get together for a charitable purpose.

You can encourage them to participate in organized annual events such as Jerry Lewis' Telethon or a March of Dimes Walkathon, or you can take on a school challenge in which only your students are going to participate.

It is one of the most
beautiful compensations of
this life that no man
can sincerely try to
help another without
helping himself.

Emerson

Progressive Publications 1996.

Seeing graffiti in some darker areas of town, a group of Art students at Platt College in Tulsa got City permission to create murals where crudeness once was. The newspapers were quick to run pictures of their work. The mayor thanked them publicly, and asked them to do more. And the students enjoyed it immensely.

Students at Dorsey Business School in Michigan dressed alike as they manned the phones for a TV Telethon. Each wore a banner across their blouses with the name of the school. They helped raise a great deal of money and at the same time showed their pride in their school.

Another school read of a poor child who could really use a motorized wheel chair. Many different events were held to raise the money. The school received ample publicity, the students really enjoyed themselves, and the needy young crippled child got his wheelchair.

Each of these activities and thousands more are initiated at campuses throughout this country each year. Without exception they help form bonds which keep students actively involved in their schools and, consequently, unlikely candidates to drop-out.

So watch the papers for a need which could use the help of many, like raising money for an operation which must be had to save a life. Then ask for students who would like to get involved. You'll see instant morale blossom and chances are your school will get some favorable press.

10. Maintain a library of books, audio tapes and

video tapes which motivate and encourage students to succeed.

Contact your local book wholesalers for copies of books such as Carnegie's *How To Win Friends and Influence People*, Norman Vincent Peale's *The Power of Positive Thinking*'or Napoleon Hill's *Think and Grow Rich*.

These are three of the best, but there are hundreds more every one of your students should read so they can stay focused on their objectives.

Then collect a library of similar type audio and video tapes as these are excellent tools which all your staff members can use to help counsel students with problems.

Even if you don't have the knowledge to act as a counselor you can get an expert's advice on tape and share it with those students who have come to you for answers.

Many excellent motivational and instructional audio and video tapes can be obtained from the wide selection offered by Nightingale Conant. You can call for their latest catalog at 1-800-323-3938 or write to:
Nightingale-Conant Corporation
P.O. Box 845
Morton Grove, IL 60053-9921

11. *Turn an unused room into a chapel or a "Thinking Room."*

Each of us has his or her own beliefs about creation and a Supreme Being.

Whether students would care to talk to a higher authority or just have a quiet place to go to sort out the answers to a problem, having a room for this purpose will be appreciated.

Keep it dimly lit, with chairs or pews to allow users to sit, stand or kneel. Avoid any statues or pictures which are affiliated with specific religions unless, of course, you are operating a private religious school.

Decor can include tranquil pictures of landscapes or seascapes, and flowers and plants, either real or artificial.

12. Create compatible living for out of town students.

If you arrange housing for students who may be leaving home for the first time, you must put a little effort into finding compatible roommates.

Look for similar backgrounds and mutual interests. Don't even think about putting a smoker with a non-smoker. Consider religious beliefs, study habits, those who must work while attending, snoring, drinking habits, ethnic backgrounds, etc.

Give every student the option of requesting a change in roommates after a trial period.

Homesickness is a real problem for many young people, so don't take this topic lightly or you will have drop-outs you could have avoided.

13. Tutoring

It is wise to set up a tutoring program as nothing causes more drop-outs than students adopting a negative attitude about their academic achievement.

Once an "I'll never make it" inkling begins to be a frequent commuter on a student's train of thought, getting off at the next station becomes a very real possibility.

If you recall, we discussed *school dollars* when we talked about paying for student trips. Well here is an excellent way to pay your more advanced students to assist those who for some reason are having a difficult time.

If you don't now have something like *School Dollars* we suggest you design them. They can also be used to get better prices at your book store, at your school restaurant, or if you are really ambitious, at local stores near your school. Often merchants are glad to accept these *school dollars* to pay up to 15% of the cost of items they sell.

You might also design a sign and make a few copies to give to merchants to display, "We accept Washington Tech. School Student Dollars for up to 15% of any purchase."

14. *Set a policy: Students don't need to verbally ask for help!*

When I was attending school, I was relatively shy and very reticent to ask a question, thinking someone might ridicule me for "asking such a dumb question."

In conversations over the years I found out I wasn't the

only one to experience this fear.

But as some people are aggressive and some aren't, you can't just say to the shy people, "Don't be shy!". It won't work.

We suggest you initiate this procedure at your school and enlist the help of all your teachers to make it work. The policy is simply: All students who need help are to remain in their seats after class until the teacher says "How can I help You?" If time isn't available then to answer the question, the teacher can set up a time to meet later.

If you have teachers who refuse to participate, record any conversations you may have with the teacher, have them sign a paper if possible, and seek every means you can discover to get rid of them.

As I see it, no school in this country can afford to have teachers standing in front of classrooms who don't sincerely care about the success of all students. Find a way to say goodbye.

15. Create extra-curricular activities.

Everyone on the school payroll should be encouraged to help students establish teams, clubs, organizations, or activities such as student plays, and subsequently act as directors, monitors and supervisors. If possible, see to it no one who wants to participate is denied membership or participation. Just about anyone can play the cymbals.

The more activities a student is involved in, the less likely it will be that he or she will drop-out.

16. *Students are more likely to stick around if they understand how your school is playing an integral part in their ultimate success.*

As I look back over my lifetime, there are numerous things I truly wish I had learned earlier in life. Heading that list is a *FORMULA FOR SUCCESS* which I finally found and have used successfully ever since.

It appears on the next page. Enlarge it on your copy machine and be generous spreading it around. If you would like to have a laminated poster of this great advice, call the publisher and order a copy.

What is so fascinating about this formula is that it can not fail. That's why no student should go through school without being introduced to the simplicity of this dynamic prescription for achievement.

Study it yourself, then assist every student you can to establish goals and thereafter stay focused.

Students simply won't drop out if they feel they are on a specific road to a desirable objective and reaching that objective can only be achieved if they graduate from your school.

Taking on the responsibility of passing on the "Formula For Success" can create some interesting predicaments, however, as I well found out.

One day, as I was passing through one of the shop areas at my Auto Mechanic school, I noticed a student standing with his hands in his pockets watching other students working. After observing him for a while, and wondering how we ever allowed this guy to enroll, I

THE FORMULA FOR SUCCESS

Throughout the entire history of mankind it has become apparent that those extraordinary men and women who are renowned for their accomplishments, all had something in common: A plan that included five major points. We pass them on to you here. Use them with all your might and you cannot fail. Only one prerequisite is necessary; your goal must be realistically believable.

"Anything the Mind Can Conceive, and Believe, Can be Achieved!"

If you intend to succeed at anything in your lifetime, you must have a plan.

HERE ARE THE FIVE POINTS OF THE SUCCESS FORMULA

1. ESTABLISH A BELIEVABLE GOAL. WRITE IT DOWN.
Be specific about the details of your plan and record the date when you intend to accomplish your goal. It is necessary to provide a "DEADLINE" for yourself.

2. VISUALIZE YOURSELF ALREADY HAVING ACCOMPLISHED YOUR GOAL.
We become what we think about. Throughout each day, you must continually take the time to dream. The more you concentrate on what it will be like when your goal is realized, the more the details of your plan will fall into place. To keep this idea alive, we suggest you make a "THINGS I MUST DO TODAY" list every day from now on. Do this either at night before retiring, or the first thing in the morning. After you get in the habit of doing this, you will find that you will accomplish twice as much in the course of your working day.

3. MAINTAIN A POSITIVE ATTITUDE.
We suggest three methods:

A. Associate only with those who also are optimists. Rid your environment of those pessimists who constantly say "I CAN'T," or who tell you "YOU'LL NEVER DO IT." Share your dreams with your positive thinking friends.

B. Use a concept which many have titled: "AUTOSUGGESTION." It is simply the procedure of repeating a positive statement over and over again. The mind is capable of amazing feats. Somehow it allows us to be what we think about if we continually make a statement. Muhammed Ali transformed himself into the Heavyweight Champion of the World by repeating "I AM THE GREATEST." Tom Monaghan brought his struggling Domino's Pizza Company to world prominence by saying "I AM GOING TO BE THE BEST PIZZA MAKER IN THE WORLD." Try it. It works.

C. Take 15 minutes a day to read some self-improvement books. There are many of them on the market, but to get started, try *The Power of Positive Thinking* by Norman Vincent Peale, or *Think and Grow Rich* by Napoleon Hill. They are two of the best and you shouldn't have any difficulty finding them at any library or bookstore.

4. PERSEVERE. DON'T ALLOW YOURSELF TO GIVE UP.
Sure, you will encounter problems, but refuse to let them get you down. Have the courage to pick yourself up after every set-back, readjust your plan, and start again. Remember that failure is a great teacher, and that *"In every adversity, there is the equivalent of an equal or greater benefit."* If you maintain this attitude, you ultimately will succeed. Almost all failures that occur are the result of somebody giving up, or not being adequately prepared for the battle. Persevere.

5. WORK-WORK-WORK-WORK-WORK
You can't very well dream up clever ways to make a million, and then work a six hour day implementing your ideas. Nothing is that simple. If you want to succeed, forget about working average hours. There is a price to pay for success and it is an unrelenting, uncompromising, uncommon effort.

Progressive Publications© Copyright 1996.

To receive a poster catalog call (352) 382-1452   No. 042

asked him to come to my office.

I introduced myself, asked him his name and his age, and invited him to sit down. I then asked him why he was here? "My Dad thought it was a good idea." was his answer. "What about your goals?", I said, then proceeded to say, "You are 21 years old, are you going to depend on your parents to think for you for the rest of your life?", "Have you given any thought to your future?", ... "What are you going to be 10 years from now?" When his answer was "31", and he wasn't kidding, I knew I had a challenge on my hands.

I spent the next few hours with this young man, giving him the fundamentals of the *Formula For Success* and how he must sit down that night without the TV on, and think as he never has before. I suggested he list every activity he likes to do, then make another list of all the professions and activities he could participate in using his most liked avocations. I challenged him to come back the following morning, having set a specific career objective. He was enthused. His eyes started to sparkle. The idea that "You can be anything you want to be" seemed to ignite his fire. "Thanks, I'll see you first thing in the morning" he said and left with the flourish of a man on a mission.

Now, I made it a habit of arriving early each morning, because that was my only time to think without interruption. Come 8 o'clock all hell breaks loose and, thereafter, my time is dictated by choosing the problem which needs solving the most.

I'm sure many of you know exactly what I mean!

Anyway, on this particular morning, I was greeted by my "Joe Klutz" as I pulled into my parking space at 5:30 A.M. I never even got out of the car, before he shouted, "I know what it is I want to be!" I said, "that's great, but what do you say we go into the school first so we can sit down and go over this?" He gave me a very enthusiastic "Sure!".

We went inside. I ushered him back to my office. I asked him to sit down. He did. I then said, "OK , tell me about your decision!"

He moved forward on his seat, his eyes got as big as saucers, and he said, with all the sincerity in the world, ... "I am going to be ... your partner!"

Frankly, I wasn't prepared for that. I sat there in silence. But finally did say, "OK, if that's what you want, you must plan every detail showing how this plan can be realized." "Present it to me and we'll go from there!"

Fortunately, his enthusiasm was short-lived, but he did begin to understand that every plan for success must include goals which are realistic.

I subsequently explained to him that a goal can't just be something we want. It must be an objective we believe we can reach. The fact that I would very much like to play shortstop next season for the Detroit Tigers is something I would love to do but hardly realistic for a man who will never see forty again and who has severe difficulty bending over to tie his shoes. He understood.

When you are passing on the "Formula" make sure

you encourage your students to be realistic, but by no means should you discourage them from being bold and adventurous.

17. DISCIPLINE!, .. Can it really be used to romance students? .... Absolutely!

Once a student is introduced to the Formula For Success, he or she usually begins to understand the need for self-discipline.

For those who don't even have what it takes to get up after hitting the snooze alarm, however, a disciplined environment must necessarily precede one's ability to discipline one's self.

So although many want discipline as they know it is a prerequisite for success, they can't apply it themselves just yet. That's where we educators come in. We must set firm rules.

Generally speaking, if we have rules and say little to those who break them, then students will just keep on breaking the rules. Only if we go nuts when a rule is broken will students sit up and take notice. What are we saying here? If you set a rule, enforce the rule, but always let the student know the reason for the rule. Let me give you an example:

At a school I owned, I wasn't at all happy with the attendance percentages. Consequently, I established an attendance policy which was actually absurd:

ATTENDANCE POLICY

AS A GENERAL RULE, ABSENCE IS NOT ALLOWED.

ABSENCE IS ONLY PERMITTED WHEN THERE IS A DEATH IN THE FAMILY. AND THAT DEATH IS YOURS.

We backed up the policy, by making it very difficult for students to just show up in class. Following any absence a student had to fill out a form and go through two interviews.

Didn't this procedure make students mad? No, because every student in attendance knew that following the rules was in their best interest.

At orientation and thereafter we stressed this message: "When we accepted you as a student, we accepted the obligation of training you to the best of our abilities so we can get you the best job possible." As you can't learn when you are not here, you prevent us from doing our best to give you the education necessary to get you the best job we can."

"When employers call here for our graduates, they naturally want the most skilled person we can send, but if they are paying top wages they can afford to be fussy, so they want more than just a skilled worker." "They want someone who is going to show up every day, ... and on time." "That's why they invariably ask, "What's the student's attendance look like?" "Know what?, we don't lie to them."

"So if we allowed you to be absent, we would in effect be saying we don't care if you get a good paying job or not!" "Well that's just not so!" "And that is why we have this attendance policy."

So does discipline romance students? Absolutely! Our rate of attendance improved dramatically after we initiated our Attendance Policy. We think yours will, too, as long as your students fully understand the reason for the *rule.*

Another example of our reaction to breaking the rules was our reaction to finding graffiti in a stall in a rest room. We rang the alarm bell 12 times. Every instructor called an immediate halt to everything going on in their classrooms. Everyone was asked to immediately assemble in the main shop area. There was no doubt in anyone's mind that a very serious matter was about to be discussed. *What's happening was written on every student's face.*

We then started out as follows: "In order to get all our students the best jobs possible, we constantly invite employers to visit us." "Their reaction is almost always positive, unless they have been given reason to believe our students are irresponsible slobs who don't give a damn about caring for their employer's premises."

"This morning, some stupid student sent such a message by writing his foul thoughts on the wall in a rest room."

"Frankly, we hope you can see how damaging such an act is to all of us, for the success of this school is directly tied to the success of each student."

"We cannot afford to have any employer walk away from a visit here with a negative feeling, so please do whatever you can to project a professional image."

"Every student and every member of our staff and faculty carries the entire reputation of this school on his or her shoulders." "Do your best to uphold this image, and we promise to do the very best we can to assist you to get a better job."

"Thank you for your attention and your under-standing!"

18. You will be romancing your students when you provide dynamic instruction.

Certainly one of the tragedies of our school system is that a "boring" teacher who is protected by tenure will continue to "turn kids off" rather than on, for as long as signed documents so state. This is sad. For if heart and one's ability to pass on knowledge were the fore-most requirements for a license to teach, our nation would have far fewer problems than we have now.

If the truth were known, teachers would be high on the list of *Causes of Attrition.*

I am from the school which says "there is no such thing as a dull subject, ... just dull teachers."

Make sure your students look forward to coming to class.

A) Make sure you tell your students what is coming up next. Tell them what you know. Then tell them what you told them. In other words, plan and be organized.

B) Never operate the same way on two consecutive days. Teach by drawing on the floor while the students are standing on tables. Reverse the pro-cedure the next day, have the students sit on the floor. Hold class in the park or the parking lot. Use tapes, drawings, show and tell, costumes, charts, guest speakers, the joke of the day, movement, field trips, competitive games such as Jeopardy, shout, whisper, sing, show video tapes, etc.

Make your class exciting, .. whatever the subject.

C) Have a suggestion box sitting in your room and solicit ideas for making your class more dynamic. Award simple prizes for creativity which conveys ideas relevant to the subject matter.

D) Use competition. Choose teams to compete. Challenge teams to come up with questions to stump the other teams. Put weak students with stronger students from whom they can learn.

Losing teams must bow down before the members of the winning teams and say something silly like "Oh Master, you are indeed a wonderful, brilliant, person and I am not worthy of standing in your shadow." Or you can have the losers push peanuts across the floor using only their noses, or some other such nonsense.

Just make sure that whenever competitive games are held everyone agrees in advance what each member of the losing team must do. In fact, it is not a bad idea to have the teams themselves come up with the "agony of defeat."

At one school I know of it was common practice that the members of the losing team washed the cars of the members of the winning team.

E) Have fun. You as a teacher can only be effective if you enjoy coming to work each day. Make this

happen. Be that teacher that students long
remember for "turning my life around."

19. Teach your students self esteem, ... that each of them is special, ... so special, that they are unique in all the world.

The direct result of low self-esteem is often dropping-
out of school. As educators, we must strive to make
everybody feel they are capable of great achievement
and certainly not dependent on others to give them a
handout or make them feel that they belong.

On the following pages are some of the posters
developed by Progressive Publications to make every
student realize that:

Regardless if a person is poor, he or she cannot use
that as an excuse, .. *THE WORLD IS AGAINST ME.*

That we will progress through life achieving as long as
we don't use that ugly work, ... *CAN'T*

That we never allow ourselves to be influenced by our
peers if it means luring us down a path we will someday regret traveling, ... *SING YOUR OWN SONG*

Continually encourage every one of your students to
share their goals with you in one-on-one sessions. This
will give you the opportunity to sell yourself so that no
student feels .... "Nobody believes in me."

Sad as it may seem, many parents have little
communication with their children. And in many cases
it is far less than the parents think it is. Usually, the
reason is that the parents continually convey the

THE WORLD IS AGAINST ME

"THE world is against me," he said with a sigh.
"Somebody stops every scheme that I try.
The world has me down and it's keeping me there;
I don't get a chance. Oh, the world is unfair!
When a fellow is poor then he can't get a show;
The world is determined to keep him down low."

"What of Abe Lincoln?" I asked. "Would you say
That he was much richer than you are to-day?
He hadn't your chance of making his mark,
And his outlook was often exceedingly dark;
Yet he clung to his purpose with courage most grim
And he got to the top. Was the world against him?

"What of Ben Franklin? I've oft heard it said
That many a time he went hungry to bed.
He started with nothing but courage to climb,
But patiently struggled and waited his time.
He dangled awhile from real poverty's limb,
Yet he got to the top. Was the world against him?

I could name you a dozen, yes, hundreds, I guess,
Of poor boys who've patiently climbed to success;
All boys who were down and who struggled alone,
Who'd have thought themselves rich if your fortune
    they'd known;
Yet they rose in the world you're so quick to condemn,
And I'm asking you now, was the world against them?

Edgar A. Guest

Progressive Publications 1996.   To receive a poster catalog call (352) 382-1452   No. 034

CAN'T

Can't is the worst word that's written or spoken;
  Doing more harm here than slander and lies;
On it is many a strong spirit broken,
  And with it many a good purpose dies.
It springs from the lips of the thoughtless each morning
  And robs us of courage we need through the day:
It rings in our ears like a timely-sent warning
  And laughs when we falter and fall by the way.

Can't is the father of feeble endeavor,
  The parent of terror and half-hearted work;
It weakens the effects of artisans clever,
  And makes of the toiler an indolent shirk.
It poisons the soul of the man with a vision,
  it stifles in infancy many a plan;
It greets honest toiling with open derision
  And mocks at the hopes and the dreams of a man.

Can't is a word none should speak without blushing;
  To utter it should be a symbol of shame;
Ambition and courage it daily is crushing;
  It blights a man's purpose and shortens his aim.
Despise it with all of your hatred of error;
  Refuse it the lodgment it seeks in your brain;
Arm against it as a creature of terror,
  And all that you dream of you some day shall gain.

Can't is the word that is foe to ambition,
  An enemy ambushed to shatter your will;
Its prey is forever the man with a mission
  And bows but to courage and patience and skill.
Hate it, with hatred that's deep and undying,
  For once it s welcomed 'twill break any man;
Whatever the goal you are seeking, keep trying
  And answer this demon by saying: "I can"

Edgar A. Guest

Progressive Publications 1996.   To receive a poster catalog call (352) 382-1452   No. 022

SING YOUR OWN SONG

Don't just agree ...
So you can belong,

Peer pressure is ...
Very often wrong.

Stand firm for what's right,
... Gather your might,

And when asked to be stupid,
... Be strong!

Arrendee

Believe In Yourself

Believe in yourself and in your dream
Though impossible things may seem.

Someday, somehow, you'll get through
To the goal you have in view.

Mountains fall and seas divide,
Before the one who in his stride,

Takes a hard road day by day,
sweeping obstacles away.

Believe in yourself and in your plan.
Say not, I cannot, but I can.

The prizes of life we fail to win,
Because we doubt the power within.

Anonymous

Progressive Publications 1996.

message to their kids that they are "useless", "irresponsible", "lazy", "stupid", and furthermore "You'll never amount to anything, you bum."

Then after filling their children's heads with all this negative baggage they have given them to lug around, they scream at them for how poorly they are performing in school.

That's why it is necessary that we as educators must step in to provide the "You can do it" stuff that is often never mentioned at home.

If you would like laminated copies of the posters which appear in this book order them from the publisher. If not, you have our permission to blow up copies of them on your copy machine and give them to anyone you feel they will help.

20. Make a conscious effort to see to it that no student is ever embarrassed in front of classmates.

Our research on drop-outs, which we have performed now for many years, has revealed that far more students drop out following an embarrassing moment in class than you could possibly imagine.

In effect, this is the opposite of romancing.

Now logic tells us that teachers should never criticize, condemn or insult a student in front of the entire class and yet it happens every day in thousands of classrooms.

Being humiliated is never easy for anyone to accept, but when it happens before an audience of our peers it is a reason for resentment. Some will fight back, but for most, it is good reason to say goodbye.

I have gone to many homes to apologize for the ignorance of "a careless statement" made by a member of the faculty. Less than half I was able to get to return to school, and of these, most only agreed after I assured them they would not have to attend a class taught by the teacher that offended them.

If you are an administrator, let it be known that any teacher found guilty of embarrassing a student while other classmates are present, will be severely disciplined, if not dismissed.

If you as a teacher are frustrated with a particular student, request that the student meet with you after class. If the matter can't be solved in a private conversation, consult supervision and ask for their assistance. But don't let your temper get the best of you by attacking a student during class.

21. *Whenever given the opportunity, treat students as peers.*

If you haven't read Dale Carnegie's *How To Win Friends And Influence People* lately, maybe it's time for a refresher course. I pick it up frequently because the wisdom in this book never grows old. Just my memory does.

One of the gems advocated in this guide is "Giving A Person A Reputation To Live Up To." I suggest you use it with your students every opportunity you have.

At seminars, this part of the program is always

with role playing. Volunteers play the roles of a faculty member and a student. I play the role of another faculty member.

The scene opens as I am talking to a student about whatever, when another faculty member approaches (Jim). I immediately stop talking to the student and acknowledge Jim with a hearty hello. I then turn back to the student and say, "Listen, I'll have to talk to you at some other time." With that I promptly turn my back on the student and walk away with Jim.

What we have illustrated is a common practice which conveys a message to the student which says, "You are insignificant" and "I've got more important things to do than talk to someone like you!"

Having visited schools all around this country, I can tell you that without exception, the best schools are those where every student feels that the faculty members are their peers, and that together, they are working to achieve a common goal: a meaningful education.

So the second scene in our role playing session goes like this: As Jim approaches, I say, "Jim, I'd like you to meet Mary Smith, who because of her rare abilities, just might be the first female President of the United States." "Nobody works harder at their studies than Mary does." "Mary, Jim and I are going to lunch, would you care to join us?"

Now asking your students to go to lunch is certainly not necessary, but taking advantage of every opportunity to give a student a reputation to live up to should be.

If you use this concept today with waiters and waitresses, store clerks, taxi drivers, whomever, you'll find them knocking themselves out to prove your assessment of their abilities is not exaggerated.

Saying out loud, "Jim, we sure are in luck today, we've got the best waitress in all of Manhattan" will do nothing but bring you service that those at other tables aren't getting. It's just human nature! Try it, ... particularly with your students.

22. Teach your students how to be well-liked.

Everybody would like to think of themselves as popular. Those who really feel this way come to school each day anxious to meet and greet their many friends. They aren't tied up in a lonely existence with no one to talk to, consequently, they aren't likely to drop-out.

You can assist your students by providing them with the guidance which is detailed on the posters printed on the following two pages, *HOW TO BE WELL LIKED* and *TO BE RESPECTED.*

Make copies on your copy machine and distribute this advice. Perhaps we can make every student feel they are well-liked and that they have many friends on campus. It could happen! And when it does, you will have fewer drop-outs at your school.

23. Teach students how to be happy.

Now, as educators, we sure can't be responsible for making everyone happy, but we can do two things which certainly will have an effect. One: make your-

HOW TO BECOME WELL LIKED!

First you must understand that there is little benefit in striving to have everyone like you. Consider that many, seeking to serve only themselves, are incapable of giving and consequently are not worthy of your friendship.

To sell yourself so that you will have an enviable number of people choosing to call you their friend, use this advice:

1. Smile as a matter of habit. Put it on before leaving the house each day.

2. Greet new acquaintances with a sincere ... "It's a pleasure to meet you!" Look at the person you are addressing. Use a firm handshake.

3. Use the IRA Formula to remember names:
    A) I   Identify the name in your mind. If there is any doubt about spelling, ask the person to clarify it.
    B) R   Repeat the name as many times as you can in your mind and in your conversation.
    C) A   Associate the name with something. Visualize the picture you have created which reminds you of the person's name. Log it in your "theatre of the mind."
    You will impress people if you can call them by name at your second meeting.

4. In conversation, be known as a person who never criticizes, condemns, complains, or argues. You certainly can and will disagree with others, but be aware that nobody really wins an argument. When disagreeing, simply make an offer; "tell you what, whoever's wrong has to take the other out to dinner, is it a deal?" Never just tell another person he or she is wrong! You'll have few friends if you do.

5. Be a good listener. Encourage others to speak about themselves.

6. Use compliments generously. There is always something you can say which will allow the other person to have a better day. And very often the compliment is repaid in some other way we least expect.

7. Always make the other person feel as though their opinion is important to you.

8. Give the other person an image to live up to. "Well folks, we are in luck today, here comes the best waitress in Clark County!"

9. Don't partake in slander. Let it be said that you never were heard to say a bad word about anyone. Remember this: "Those who choose to damage the reputation of others, whether true or not, will have to live with the rebuttal!"

10. Always try to use empathy when listening to the opinions and problems of others. Close your eyes and see yourself as the other person. This habit is one worth developing as you are less likely to have to remove a shoe from your mouth.

"A Friend is a Gift You Give Yourself"

Progressive Publications© Copyright 1996.

To receive a poster catalog call (352) 382-1452   No. 029

TO BE RESPECTED

BE CONSIDERATE OF OTHERS ...

BRING JOY TO THOSE EXPERIENCING PROBLEMS,

CONSOLATION TO THOSE IN SORROW,

HOPE TO THOSE LINGERING IN DOUBT,

UNDERSTANDING TO THOSE WHO ARE MISUNDERSTOOD,

APOLOGIES TO THOSE YOU HAVE OFFENDED,

AND KIND WORDS TO THOSE, WHO THROUGH NO

FAULT OF THEIR OWN, ARE SLANDERED AND RIDICULED.

THROUGHOUT YOUR LIFETIME, THOSE WHO PROUDLY

CALL YOU THEIR FRIEND WILL SEE TO IT ...

NO WEEDS GROW ON THE PATH TO YOUR DOOR.

To receive a poster catalog call (352) 382-1452   No. 080

self an example of what being happy should look like. Two: assist your students to schedule, then anticipate enjoyable goals and objectives, from just going to the movies next Friday night, to that "Ideal Job" which is just down the road.

No one has ever committed suicide while they are eagerly awaiting a happy time, a favorable experience, an exotic vacation, etc.

The poem on the next page tells it as it is, the key to being happy is forgetting bad times and concentrating on all the great things which are coming.

Make copies of this work on your copy machine and keep them handy to pass out to everyone who looks like they ate worms for breakfast. If you would like a laminated poster for permanent display, contact the publisher.

CREATING HAPPINESS

When life seems void of happiness,
Put a fond goal in view,
Cause all of us need pleasant thoughts,
Of things to look forward to.

Without a plan, a place to go,
A hoped for destination,
We often lapse into despair
And blaspheme all creation.

Worst of all we concentrate
On good times long gone by
And pity ourselves with "never again,"
"No matter what I try."

In contrast, when we look ahead,
Engrossed in positive thought,
We become our own wise teachers
And our lessons are self-taught.

So startin' now, prevent despair
Plan both work and play.
Set your sights and never give up
And joy will come your way.

Your key is anticipation,
You must never be without it.
For only then can smiles prevail
There's just no doubt about it!

Arrendee

To receive a poster catalog call (352) 382 1452   No. 031

CHAPTER 6

USING THE RECOGNITION FACTOR TO INFLUENCE STUDENTS

1. *There is no word any person would rather hear than his or her own name!*

Why do big nightclubs go out of business while the neighborhood bar continues to prosper year after year?, the beer they serve?, the shuffleboard and pool tables?, the big hamburger they serve? ...... NO!

Like the words in the *Cheers* theme song says, it's where "everybody knows your name."

I have often advocated having two schools housing 250 students each, rather than one school housing 500 students. Why? Simply because of the intimate personal communication that is possible when every staff and faculty member in a school knows every student by name.

If you are a school administrator, consider the following ideas regardless of how many students are in your school.

A) Prior to the start of a new class or semester, urge all your faculty members to study the pictures of all students which we hope you have adhered to the exterior of the student files. If you haven't done this please consider it soon. The investment will pay for itself.

B) Hold contests with your faculty members to see who can remember the most names. Have as a goal: Every staff and faculty member knows the name of every student in the school.

C) Greet all students by name that first day of class. It will make a lasting impression.

D) A sign at the entrance to your school on the first day of class will also do much to make a good first impression. Under a heading which might read something like, *WELCOME V.I.P.'S OF THE FUTURE*, you have an individual picture of all new students, their names, and personal information which includes the school they came from, their hobbies, and the career objectives they intend to achieve.

Usually, the names of the prominent students and the trouble-makers are the only ones everyone knows, while it is "What's his name" who drops out. Change this at your school. Everyone must be made to feel important, and that type of concern can only happen when everyone is addressed by his or her name.

2. *The use of praise*

When you praise an individual student you offer recognition which will keep him or her wanting more. That being so, we can assume that few students who are frequently praised will drop-out.

So in addition to greeting others with their name, find something nice to say which will make them feel good and help them to have a better day.

IT IS NICE
TO BE IMPORTANT

BUT IT IS
MORE IMPORTANT
TO BE NICE!

To receive a poster catalog call (352) 382-1452   No. 04

There is always something nice you can say. Find it!
Even after viewing the "ugliest baby on earth" you can
turn to the parents and say "He sure looks healthy and
happy, you sure are lucky!"

Putting kind words on paper is also a habit you should
get into.

When handing back tests or papers which include your
handwritten opinions following the grade, try to avoid
scribbling, "STUPID!, STUPID!, STUPID!" after a grade
of 20%. It may very well be an accurate assessment of
the student's work, but hardly a message which will
inspire the recipient to do better. You might just as well
write, "DROP OUT, DUMMY!" as this could very well be
the result of your disgust.

As we said earlier in this book, we can't just say good
riddance to those who aren't performing or giving us
problems.

How about a note on that same paper which reads:
"20%. Bob, as I see it, this grade is just about 80% short
of the potential grade I know you are capable of
getting!" "You know as well as I do that you are far too
talented to settle for being one fifth as good as you
should be." Next time I want to write *WOW!* on the
top of your paper. How about it?"

3. *Make good use of awards*

Awards can accomplish a great deal for your school.
They motivate both the recipients of the awards and
others who when seeing the Awards Ceremony, say to
themselves, "I can do that."

The cost of typesetting original copies of numerous awards is small when compared with the benefits. And you can buy fancy bordered blank award paper so that all you need to do is position the master keyline in a copy machine and create one award at a time.

At schools I have owned we have used awards to recognize students for numerous accomplishments. Among them:

- Excellent Attendance Award
- Perfect Attendance Award
- Best Appearance Award
- Most Likely To Succeed Award
- Most Congenial Award
- The Effort Award
- Top Technician Award
- Notable Achievement Award
- Best Typist Award
- Best Smile Award
- Most Considerate Award
- Most Improved Student Award
- Public Speaking Award
- School Assistance Award
- Dean's List Award
- Personality Award
- Humanitarian Award

Samples of how these awards might look are printed on the following pages.

If at all possible, hand out these awards at student assemblies. It becomes "no big deal" for anyone to receive an award, if it is sent to you through the mail or given one on one in the privacy of somebody's office.

It's like saying, "We are giving you this very special

The Management and Faculty of

_____

Proudly Presents This

EXCELLENT ATTENDANCE AWARD

to

_____

Having attended no less than 95% of all scheduled classes

From _____ to _____

Presented this _____ day of _____ 19 ___

_____   _____
Signed for Management   Signed for Faculty

The Management and Faculty of

_____

Proudly Presents This

PERFECT ATTENDANCE AWARD

to

_____

Having attended all scheduled classes

From _____ to _____

Presented this _____ day of _____ 19 ___

_____   _____
Signed for Management   Signed for Faculty

The Management and Faculty of

_____

Proudly Presents This

BEST APPEARANCE AWARD

to

_____

Having been judged so by both students and faculty

Over the period from _____ to _____

Presented this _____ day of _____ 19 ___

_____   _____
Signed for Management   Signed for Faculty

The Management and Faculty of

_____

Proudly Presents This

MOST LIKELY TO SUCCEED AWARD

to

_____

Having been judged so by both students and faculty

Over the period from _____ to _____

Presented this _____ day of _____ 19 ___

_____   _____
Signed for Management   Signed for Faculty

The Management and Faculty of

_____

Proudly Presents This

MOST CONGENIAL AWARD

to

_____

Having been judged so by both students and faculty

Over the period from _____ to _____

Presented this _____ day of _____ 19 _____

_____   _____
Signed for Management   Signed for Faculty

The Management and Faculty of

_____

Proudly Presents This

EFFORT AWARD

to

_____

Having been judged so by both Staff and Faculty

Over the period from _____ to _____

Presented this _____ day of _____ 19 ___

_____   _____
Signed for Management   Signed for Faculty

82

The Management and Faculty of

Proudly Presents This

TOP TECHNICIAN AWARD

to

Having shown outstanding ability by

Over the period from _____ to _____

Signed for Management

Signed for Faculty

The Management and Faculty of

_____

Proudly Presents This

NOTABLE ACHIEVEMENT AWARD

to

_____

Having been judged so by Staff and Faculty for

_____

Presented this _____ day of _____ 19 ___

_____
Signed for Management

_____
Signed for Faculty

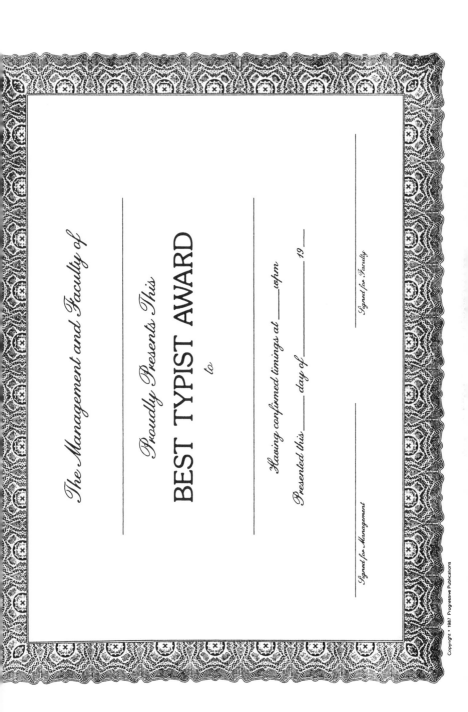

The Management and Faculty of

_____

Proudly Presents This

BEST TYPIST AWARD

to

_____

Having conformed timings at _____ wpm

Presented this _____ day of _____ 19 ____

Signed for Management _____

Signed for Faculty _____

The Management and Faculty of

_____

Proudly Presents This

BEST SMILE AWARD

to

_____

Having been judged so by both students and faculty

Over the period from _____ to _____

Presented this _____ day of _____ 19 _____

_____   _____
Signed for Management   Signed for Faculty

The Management and Faculty of

Proudly Presents This

MOST CONSIDERATE AWARD

to

Having been judged so by both students and faculty

Over the period from _____ to _____

Presented this _____ day of _____ 19 ____

Signed for Management

Signed for Faculty

The Management and Faculty of

_____

Proudly Presents This

to

MOST IMPROVED STUDENT AWARD

_____

Having shown outstanding academic improvement by

_____

Over the period from _____ to _____

_____   _____
Signed for Management   Signed for Faculty

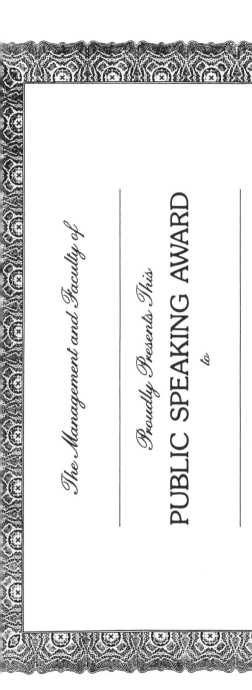

The Management and Faculty of

_____

Proudly Presents This

PUBLIC SPEAKING AWARD

to

_____

Having been judged in competition

Presented this _____ day of _____ 19 _____

_____
Signed for Management

_____
Signed for Faculty

The Management and Faculty of

_____

Proudly Presents This

SCHOOL ASSISTANCE AWARD

to

_____

For extraordinary service to this school

Over the period from _____ to _____

Presented this _____ day of _____ 19 ___

_____   _____
Signed for Management   Signed for Faculty

90

The Management and Faculty of

Proudly Presents This

DEAN'S LIST AWARD

to

Having an overall grade average of _____

For the period from _____ to _____

Presented this _____ day of _____ 19 _____

_____
Signed for Management

_____
Signed for Faculty

The Management and Faculty of

Proudly Presents This

PERSONALITY AWARD

to

Having been judged so by both students and faculty

Over the period from _____ to _____

Presented this _____ day of _____ 19___

_____ _____
Signed for Management   Signed for Faculty

The Management and Faculty of

_____

Proudly Presents This

HUMANITARIAN AWARD

to

_____

Having been judged so by students and faculty

For voluntary assistance to other students

Presented this _____ day of _____ 19 ___

_____
Signed for Management

_____
Signed for Faculty

93

award but we would appreciate it if nobody knew about it!"

Gaining the admiration and respect of good friends and associates is the reward for receiving an award. Don't deny an award recipient these benefits by holding the presentation in a broom closet.

4. *Bulletin boards can serve many purposes and are ideal for using recognition to motivate.*

I have often heard School Administrators say "Oh! students never read bulletin boards" then when I take a look at what they have posted I see such things as "VOTE FOR DEWEY", "ABACUS FOR SALE BY ORIGINAL OWNER", or "DOWN WITH PROHIBITION!"

Of course students won't read bulletin boards if you don't change them frequently and list items of interest. But I guarantee you that they will if you post articles and lists that are loaded with recognition and you change them at dependable intervals, like every Monday.

Let me give you some examples of headlines for articles:

- BIRTHDAYS COMING UP
- THOSE WHO ARE NOW ELIGIBLE TO TAKE THE STUDENT CRUISE
- THE FOLLOWING STUDENTS INCREASED THEIR TYPING SPEEDS BY 10 WPM OR MORE DURING THE MONTH OF JUNE
- RECENT STUDENT AWARDS PRESENTED
- PRIZES TO BE GIVEN TO THE WINNERS OF THE UPCOMING ATTENDANCE LOTTERY

1. Karate Lessons donated by Henry Lee.
2. A catered meal for 4 prepared by Student Chefs.
3. NBA Basketball donated by Jones Hardware.
4. A car wash arranged and done by the faculty member of your choice.
5. The audio cassette or CD of your choice presented by Holiday Sound, Inc.

NEW STORES SIGN UP TO ACCEPT OUR SCHOOL DOLLARS. IN ALPHABETICAL ORDER THEY ARE:

1. Acme Hardware
2. Bonnie's Hair Styles
3. Pizza Hut
ETC.

SIGN UP HERE TO ATTEND THE
INVESTMENT SEMINAR AUGUST 10
"HOW TO GET NO LESS THAN A 10% RETURN
BY CONSISTENTLY CHOOSING THE
RIGHT STOCKS"

1. _____
2. _____
3. _____

WINNERS OF THE "BEST MEALS IN 10 MINUTES"
RECIPE CONTEST

Use your imagination to keep your students interested in school activities and interested in knowing who is doing what around your campus. Recognition creates continuing participation. Use it generously.

5. *Your student newspaper. Another vehicle for recognition which can produce more new*

***students for your school than any advertising
piece or catalog.***

If you list all the things you put on your bulletin boards
and in addition pay homage to counselors at other
schools, local merchants, the best employers in town,
all ongoing student projects, and then be very exact
about all the great jobs your graduates were able to get,
you'll have a paper your students will look forward to
reading.

If you have a High School paper, run stories submitted
by graduates now attending Colleges or other post-
secondary schools. Find out if they would recommend
the schools they are now attending.

If you are publishing a newspaper at a post-secondary
school make sure you send copies to all State Agencies
you deal with, all high hchool counselors in your
geographic area, all prospects who inquire about
admission, all merchants who participate in your
"School Dollars" program and other school activities.

Many of your students have never gained any
recognition in their lives, consequently, when their
name does appear in an article for having accomplished
something, you can bet every one in the family and
even the neighborhood knows about it. When this
happens, you can be sure that student will never
subsequently drop out.

**6. *Counsel those who seek recognition by
performing acts which are detrimental to others.***

Unfortunately, in every school there are those who feel
they can't gain acclaim for academic achievement or

some other positive action, so they choose to be known as "bad" by demonstrating anti-social behavior.

They revel in their reputations of fear or abnormality and if allowed to live unchecked seek more outlandish acts to draw attention.

If you know of such people, do what you can to provide them with the concept of doing "good" to gain fame rather than continue on the road they are following.

Even gangs, when given the challenge of performing a noble effort to help the needy, have responded positively.

John Dillinger couldn't wait to read what was said about him each morning following one of his robberies. Bonnie and Clyde also loved the image they projected. But what price can you put on fame? All of them died violently.

On the following pages are a couple of posters which you can use as a format for discussion. The first is the TEN POINTS OF COMMON SENSE. The second is 10 common sense statements which can help all of us develop friendships. It is titled; TEN SUGGESTIONS FOR GETTING ALONG BETTER WITH PEOPLE.

Yes, this is another one of those touchy confrontations which any of us would rather live without, but please consider that if you don't try to help these people change their attitudes, chances are no one will.

7. Teach your students to realize that recognition for achievement only comes to those who

Ten Points of Common Sense

1. You cannot bring about prosperity by discouraging thrift.
2. You cannot strengthen the weak by weakening the strong.
3. You cannot help small men by tearing down big men.
4. You cannot help the poor by destroying the rich.
5. You cannot lift the wage earner by pulling down the wage payer.
6. You cannot keep out of trouble by spending more than your income.
7. You cannot further the brotherhood of man by inciting class hatred.
8. You cannot establish sound security on borrowed money.
9. You cannot build character and courage by taking away a man's initiative and independence.
10. You cannot help men permanently by doing for them what they could and should do for themselves.

William J. H. Boetcker

TEN SUGGESTIONS FOR GETTING ALONG BETTER WITH PEOPLE

1. Guard your tongue. Say less than you think.

2. Make promises sparingly. Keep them faithfully.

3. Never let an opportunity pass to say a kind word.

4. Be interested in others, their pursuits, work, families.

5. Be cheerful. Don't dwell on minor aches and small disappointments.

6. Keep an open mind. Discuss but don't argue. Disagree without being disagreeable.

7. Discourage gossip. It's destructive.

8. Be careful of others' feelings.

9. Pay no attention to ill-natured remarks about you. Live so that nobody will believe them.

10. Don't be anxious about getting credit. Just do your best and be patient.

To receive a poster catalog call (352) 382-1452   No. 088

establish goals, always think "I can", and who never give up!

Whether it is winning a medal in the Olympic games, getting into the movies, or signing your name to a professional sports contract, the formula is the same.

Please notice, too, that usually the biggest of those we call "stars" are individuals we like as people. They are the ones who sign the large endorsement contracts. So as long as you are numbering the steps one should take to be famous and successful, please list "being nice" in your equation.

Another point which must be stressed is the necessity for motivational message repetition.

You can't just read some wise words one day and carry them with you forever as you would your wallet or purse. You must take that quote you love and paste it on your bathroom mirror, or on the back of your bedroom door, or perhaps on the visor in your car. Then read it daily.

On the following page you will find the verse which appeared on a plaque which was permanently on display in Arnold Palmer's den. Consider using it and offering it to others. It sure did a pretty good job for "Arnie"!

Arnold Palmer's Favorite Plaque

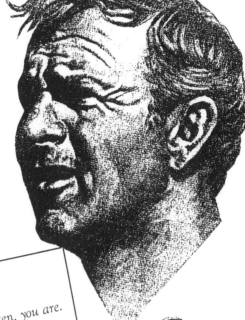

If you think you are beaten, you are.
If you think you dare not, you don't.
If you'd like to win but think you cant,
It's almost certain that you wont.
Life's battles don't always go
To the stronger woman or man,
But sooner or later, those who win
Are those who think they can.

Born September 10, 1929 · Latrobe, Pennsylvania

Progressive Publications 1996.

To receive a poster catalog call (352) 382-1452   No. 086

CHAPTER 7

USING THE MONEY FACTOR TO INFLUENCE YOUR STUDENTS

1. *Teach your students how they can retire in style*

No one at my High School bothered to tell me about the rule of 72, investing, and why I should start preparing for retirement while I was young.

Somebody thought that it was more important that I learn French. So I spent two years mastering the sentence: "Donnez-moi le parapluie s'il vous plait" which means "Please give me the umbrella."

To realize just how meaningful this was, when I finally did get to Paris for a two week stay, it never rained once.

So take it upon yourself or urge an associate to tell your students how easy it is to become millionaires if they start investing when they are young.

We have detailed just exactly how this can be done on one of our posters which appears on the next page. Enlarge it on your copy machine and pass it out, then go over the points so everyone understands.

Forty years from now, these kids will be thanking you in their daily prayers that you took the time to show them how to be independently wealthy.

How You Can Plan To Become A Millionaire And Easily Make It?

The vast majority of Americans reach retirement and have nothing to rely on other than their social security checks.

This is not only sad but absolutely avoidable. Saving when you are young and putting it away and not touching it is the secret. Follow the steps below and becoming a millionaire will definitely happen. This formula is fool proof. Here it is:

1) Understand the "Rule of 72" and that is just this: Any rate of interest divided into 72 will give you the number of years it takes for your money to double.

    Examples: (Rate of interest divided into 72)

Percentage Of Interest =		Years For Money To Double
At 5%	Your money will double in	14.4 years
At 6%	Your money will double in	12 years
At 7%	Your money will double in	10.2 years
At 8%	Your money will double in	9 years
At 9%	Your money will double in	8 years
At 10%	Your money will double in	7.2 years
At 11%	Your money will double in	6.5 years
At 12%	Your money will double in	6 years

So now you understand how important it is to shop all alternatives when you are in a position to invest. Some mutual funds have actually averaged over 12% over the span of their existence, so we are going to to use this figure to show how the magic of compound interest can make you rich.

2) Get the money you need to invest by putting your heart into your job search after you get out of school. If you work at this intelligently, it is not that difficult to get $1.00 an hour more than what is ordinarily the starting wage for the job you want.

    This is the money you are going to pledge for retirement. You promise yourself that regardless of the hand life deals you, you will not touch this money.

    How much are we talking about? Can just $1.00 per hour add up to anything substantial? Take a look: $1.00 an hour equals $40 per week, $2080.00 per year.

3) If you are 20 years old and invest $2080.00 in the mutual fund of your choice, which ultimately averages 12% interest, here is how the value of your account will grow.

Your Age	Amount of Investment	Value Of Account
20	$2080.00	$ 2,080.00
26	$2080.00	$ 4,160.00
32	$2080.00	$ 8,320.00
38	$2080.00	$ 16,640.00
44	$2080.00	$ 33,280.00
50	$2080.00	$ 66,540.00
56	$2080.00	$ 133,080.00
62	$2080.00	$ 266,160.00

You can understand that if you invest the same amount when you are 21, 22, 23, and 24 and never invest another dime, you will have an amount in the neighborhood of $1,500,000 when you reach the age of 65.

Sure, but won't inflation make this money worth far less? Yes!, but not as much as you might think. If you look back to 1950 you'll understand. You will still be in the top 5% in the nation and be independently wealthy whether social security is still with us or not

4. If you are still not sure whether you'll have enough to retire at 65 or you want to retire at a much earlier age, keep investing every year beyond your 24th Birthday.

    As long as you maintain the "hands off" approach to the money you set aside, you'll continue to gain wealth you never dreamed you could accumulate.

Bottom Line: You can plan to be wealthy and make it even if you never receive any more than a modest wage. So do it!

Progressive Publications· Copyright 1996.   To receive a poster catalog call (352) 382-1452   No. 058

Nobody knows if our Social Security system will still be functioning or not, but one thing is sure, if all the income you have to live on at retirement comes from the government, you are not going to be living high on the hog.

If you would like to have a 12" x 18" laminated copy of this poster, call or write the publisher.

2. *Using rewards for better attendance*

At one of my schools we initiated a program which was a lot of fun and very effective. The name of every student who was not late or absent during any full month was put into a lottery pot. Names were then pulled at a mass meeting and prizes were awarded.

The prizes were always on display in advance. One month the grand prize was a used car which was fixed up by the students in an Auto Mechanic School. Other prizes included an electric typewriter, two tickets to a rock concert, dinner for two at local restaurants who donated the award, a tool set donated by a vendor, and a myriad of other small gifts donated by businessmen in the neighborhood who wanted the student business.

In addition to the prizes which individuals could win we also had a *Homeroom Class Attendance Award.* The class with the highest rate of attendance was given a cash award to buy pizza, drinks, whatever, for a class party held during school hours.

Another twist to this award was that we doubled the amount of the cash award if any class had no absenteeism for an entire month. This offering led to many comic situations.

After three weeks in which no students in a class were absent, it was common to overhear a student on the phone at first break saying, "so what, you've got pneumonia, get your ass in here." The peer pressure was indeed intense.

In retrospect, I can't help but think this was a pretty unhealthy incentive to use as many students came to school coughing, wheezing, limping, etc. But the class morale that developed was awesome.

And, of course, we always announced the class attendance awards at a mass assembly, so each class could boo or cheer depending on where their percentage was on the list.

Student morale is created by getting your students involved in a wide variety of individual and group activities.

Whatever you do, don't immediately think that these types of things can't be done at your school as the head person wouldn't go for it or it's not in the budget. Look to your own students to create awards, and don't ever forget that there are businessmen, corporations and parents who will donate money or goods if they feel a "fresh approach" program is worthwhile.

3. Explain to your students the correlation between education and earnings.

Reputation is the soul of memory. Consequently, we can never remind our students too many times that education is money.

We can illustrate this in many ways, but tying grades

THE CORRELATION BETWEEN EDUCATION AND MAKING MONEY

Right now in the United States, over forty million Americans fall below the poverty line. Kids go to bed hungry, but even worse, they have considerably less chance of ever climbing out of the "cycle of poverty" ... unless they are able to stay in school until they have mastered a saleable skill or profession.

If you think you are going to be the exception to this rule, make big money without further education, please think again.

There is a direct relationship between the productive time you spend in school and the annual income you will be able to generate.

Please study the charts below, then make a commitment to continue your education until you are confident your abilities are such that others will seek your expertise.

1994 FIGURES

Years Of Education	Monthly Earnings
Didn't Finish High School	$1,199.00
Have a High School Diploma	$1,669.00
Completed 1 to 3 Years After High School	$2,166.00
Earned a Bachelor's Degree	$2,841.00
Earned A Master's Degree	$3,333.00
Earned A Doctorate Degree	$4,581.00
Earned A Professional Degree	$6,227.00

Poverty Level By Family Size As Of 1992

	Yearly Income
1 person (under age 65)	$ 7,299.00
(over age 65)	$ 6,729.00
2 persons	$ 9,137.00
3 persons	$11,186.00
4 persons	$14,335.00
5 persons	$16,952.00
6 persons	$19,137.00
7 persons	$21,594.00
8 persons	$24,053.00
9 persons or more	$28,745.00

HIT THE BOOKS

Progressive Publications⊙ Copyright 1996.   To receive a poster catalog call (352) 382-1452   No. 059

and skills to starting wages is certainly a method that readers can easily comprehend.

For any specific profession you can use a chart like this:

Earn a grade avg. of 2:00 (70%) ... Earn a wage of $15,000
Earn a grade avg. of 2:50 (78%) ... Earn a wage of $20,000
Earn a grade avg. of 3:00 (85%) ... Earn a wage of $25,000
Earn a grade avg. of 3:50 (93%) ... Earn a wage of $30,000
Earn a grade avg. of 4:00 (100%).. Earn a wage of $35,000

Here is another example of a chart I used at a Business School. See if you can design one for your students using actual starting wages provided by your Placement Department.

Type 55 words a minute ... gain a starting wage of $12,000
Type 60 words a minute ... gain a starting wage of $15,000
Type 65 words a minute ... gain a starting wage of $18,000
Type 70 words a minute ... gain a starting wage of $21,000
Type 80 words a minute ... gain a starting wage of $24,000
Type 90 words a minute ... gain a starting wage of $27,000
Type 100 words a minute . WRITE YOUR OWN FIGURE

4. *Take it upon yourself to show students how to set up a budget.*

Many students drop out of school because they are short of money. Big surprise, right? Hardly, but what may surprise you is why the shortages occured. I have personally counseled students who thought that having a stereo was far more important than paying tuition. Others who "Had to go on vacation, buy a guitar as it was once played by Elvis, hire a limousine to impress a date, etc.

Making It

If you start any course,
then finish it!
If you think you know enough,
diminish it!
Learning must never end,
continue it!
Don't say, "later man,"
get into it!
A skill is security,
learn it!
That's what allows you to
earn it!

Arrendee

Progressive Publications 1996.

For most of us, it is necessary to provide ourselves with a plan of money management. And we simply can't carry it around in our heads. It must be down on paper.

On the following pages you will find forms which are self-explanatory. You have our permission to enlarge them on your copy machine and distribute copies to your students.

Form 1 is to be used to determine all the money you will work with.

Form 2 is to be used to record all your fixed monthly expenses.

Form 3 is to be used to record your *Day to Day* expenses. As this is the area where most of us get in trouble because we "can't remember everything", it is helpful to use the following guide to jog our memories. Use it with your students in addition to a lot of scrap paper so that the figures we finally write down on the form are well-considered.

1. *Food and related items:* the amounts of your regular grocery bills; what you spend to eat out in restaurants (including tips); candy and snacks from vending machines; soft drinks, beer, wine, and liquor; cigarettes; pet foods and supplies; personal and household items such as toothpaste and cosmetics which you buy at the supermarket.

2. *Household services and expenses:* home repairs and improvements; any maintenance costs not counted in your fixed expenses; cleaning supplies; household help.

3. *Furnishings and equipment:* what you buy outright for cash and down payments for large and small appliances, glass, china, silverware, curtains, rugs, upholstering, accessories, other items.

4. *Clothes:* everything, ranging from repairs and alterations through laundry and dry cleaning to the seemingly insignificant accessories which can mount up to alarming totals.

5. *Transportation:* car repairs, tune-ups, oil changes, new tires, bus, train, taxi, and air fares, parking charges, bridge tolls.

6. *Medical care:* doctor and dentist bills not listed under your fixed expenses, drugs, eyeglasses, hospital and nursing expenses not covered by medical insurance, veterinary bills for your pets.

7. *Personal care:* the barber and hairdresser, toilet articles, cosmetics and other items not paid for by each family member's personal allowance and *not* in your supermarket bills.

8. *Education and recreation:* books, theater, movie, and concert tickets, entertaining friends, newspaper and magazine subscriptions, musical instruments and music lessons; hobby equipment, vacation and holiday expenses, the upkeep of your pleasure boat, swimming pool, or riding horse, tuition and fees not included on Form II.

9. *Gifts and contributions:* what is not paid out of personal allowances.

10. *Other things and non-things:* Only you can fill out this item.

INCOME CHART

WHAT WE WILL GET FROM	JAN.	FEB.	MAR.	APR.	MAY	JUNE	JULY	AUG.	SEPT.	OCT.	NOV.	DEC.	YEARLY TOTAL	NOTES
Husband's job														
Wife's job														
Business interests														
Interest														
Dividends														
Rent														
Gifts														
Company bonus or bonuses														
Tax refunds														
Moonlighting or jobs														
Profits from sales														
Alimony														
Govt. Grant														
Govt. Loan														
Other Loan														
Other														
Other														
Other														
Totals for the month														

FORM 2   FIXED EXPENSES — INCLUDING SAVINGS

WHAT WE MUST SPEND AND SAVE	JAN.	FEB.	MAR.	APR.	MAY	JUNE	JULY	AUG.	SEPT.	OCT.	NOV.	DEC.	YEAR'S TOTAL	NOTES
Rent or mortgage														
Fuel bills														
Telephone														
Electricity, gas														
Water														
Installment payment A														
Installment payment B														
Education Tuition & Fees														
Real estate taxes														
Income taxes														
Home and life insurance														
Auto insurance														
Medical, dental														
What we must set aside for savings alone														
Other														
Other														
Other														
Other														
Totals for each Month														

WHAT WE WILL SPEND FOR DAY-TO-DAY LIVING THIS MONTH	JAN.	FEB	MAR.	APR.	MAY	JUNE	JULY	AUG.	SEPT.	OCT.	NOV.	DEC.	NOTES
For food and related items	$	$	$	$	$	$	$	$	$	$	$	$	
For household services and expenses													
For furnishings and equipment													
For clothes.													
For transportation													
For medical care													
For personal care													
For education and recreation													
For gifts and contributions													
For other things and non-things													
For other things and non-things													
For other things and non-things													
TOTAL	$	$	$	$	$	$	$	$	$	$	$	$	
Total available for the month (from last line of form III)										$	$	$	

113

One last item worth mentioning. Nothing destroys a budget more than a credit card in the hands of an undisciplined user. Strongly suggest that all credit cards be cut in two until later in life when budgetting is not essential. Provide the scissors. Hold a ceremony.

CHAPTER 8

USING THE SELF-PRESERVATION FACTOR TO INFLUENCE STUDENTS

1. BEFRIEND AND ASSIST THOSE WHO ARE VICTIMS OF PHYSICAL ABUSE, AND THOSE WHO ARE SUBJECT TO BECOMING VICTIMS.

    Back in the 1980's I ran a degree granting college in California. Shortly after I arrived there I explained to both the staff and faculty that I was a fanatic about retention and solicited their help in creating a campus attitude of caring.

    After asking that each of the employees assume the role of a counselor whenever they felt their experiences could help, I further requested that they take on the responsibility of knowing who to refer students to if in their opinion expert guidance was needed.

    Then I asked that every student who was absent more than two consecutive days be sent to me before they were allowed to return to class. Knowing that far too many drop-outs occur after students are out for a few days and then a few more days, I wanted to make sure each student was mentally and physically prepared to resume their studies. It also gave me a great opportunity to practice a wide variety of pep talks.

    Now, although I had suspected that California students were a little more expressive than those found back in

How to Avoid Abusive Relationships

The warning signs of a controlling relationship often appear as early as the first date. The signs might not be as frequent or as severe when dating as it is with married couples, but don't fool yourself.

All abusive relationships have one thing in common: Without help, the abuse will happen more often and more severely, up to the point of critical injury or even death.

So you will be able to stop a relationship before it gets to the point you are in serious trouble, here is s list of danger signs. Any combination of these signs should tell you "Get out of this relationship before it's too late."

- *Shows jealousy.*
- *Keeps you "all to himself" (or herself). Puts down your family and friends.*
- *Criticizes you and your opinions, makes all of the decisions.*
- *Makes you feel that he or she "Knows more than you."*
- *Dictates use of your time and money.*
- *Throws, breaks, kicks, and punches objects when angry.*
- *Drinks alcohol excessively or uses drugs.*
- *Calls you names.*
- *Threatens you with words, looks, or gestures.*
- *Tells you about past violent experiences with others.*
- *Blames other people for his or her problems in life.*
- *Tells you that his or her violence, shouting, or anger is your fault.*
- *Has strict ideas about "a man's job" or "a woman's job."*
- *Has you on alert at all times as to how you have to act or what you can say.*
- *Goes overboard to say he or she is sorry after a blowup.*
- *Controls children with fear, threats and punishment.*

If you find yourself saying "yes" to 3 or more of the list above, but feel you can effect a change ... think again. Zebras don't change their stripes and neither do people who are prone to abusing others. Say Good-bye!

Progressive Publications© Copyright 1996.

To receive a poster catalog call (352) 382-1452   No. 065

the mid-west, I was not prepared for what I was about to experience: one girl after another who came in with broken arms and legs, black eyes and bruises everywhere, the victims of husbands and boy friends who were sick, heartless abusers.

Despite the obvious cruelty shown, however, few of these women said they would even consider leaving "the man" in their lives. In fact, the majority actually blamed themselves, feeling that they were at fault for getting their man angry.

I was quick to determine that I wasn't qualified to handle these sessions as logic was a useless tool. I went looking for experts who were experienced with this problem, knew what to say to these victims and knew how to arrange for new housing where the man in their lives couldn't find them.

I urge you to do the same as this scenario is far more common than you may think. If this isn't a priority at your school, you can bet that drop-outs due to abuse will continue to rise on your list of "Reasons for Attrition."

To assist all your students to avoid Relationships which could lead to abuse, study the material on the poster which appears on the opposite page.

Is this material also appropriate for males? Certainly. Although I never have had a guy come to me to complain about female abuse, I am sure it does happen. Keep in mind that abuse does not necessarily have to be physical. Mental abuse can be equally painful.

If you would care to have a laminated 18" x 12" poster

titled, HOW TO AVOID ABUSIVE RELATIONSHIPS, order it from the publisher.

By posting this information you will help all your students avoid getting involved in abusive relationships, and keep them concentrating on their studies.

Students involved in abusive relationships will often end up dropping out, as each hour of every day they are preoccupied with fear.

If you suspect that a student you know is a victim, don't hesitate to get involved. You may save a student and possibly a life.

2. MAKE SURE THAT IGNORANCE OF AIDS OR SOME OTHER DISEASE DOESN'T PANIC YOUR STUDENTS CAUSING SOME TO DROP-OUT.

Back in the seventies when AIDS was just surfacing as the severe problem it is, rumors as to how you could catch it were as numerous as excuses for being absent from school.

About this time, a friend of mine who owned a Proprietary Business School had a heart attack and asked me to assist at his school. I accepted the job and loved it up until the day one of the few male students on campus was written up in the local paper as a leader in the effort to raise more money for AIDS research. In the article it was disclosed that our student was HIV positive.

All hell broke loose. Students started asking for refunds of their tuition. Others demanded the student be dismissed. Others simply disappeared, never to be seen again. All this because of ignorance, as no real threat existed, but it did result in a moral dilemma and the swallowing of a lot of Excedrin.

As it turned out, the student resigned, and dedicated the remainder of his life to helping others. Had it not been so, however, the question remained, ... did we have the right to ask him to leave? I don't think so!

Now today, most people are very well educated about AIDS but I would suggest you take every precaution at your school to make sure your students know about contracting this or any disease which might surface sometime in the future.

On the following page is a poster on AIDS. Enlarge it on your copy machine and make sure all students get a copy, or order a laminated copy of this poster from the publisher and keep it on permanent display.

The fear of contracting a disease can result in chaos. Make "an ounce of prevention is worth a pound of cure" a motto at your school. Educate before ignorance causes you a very expensive headache.

3. PREJUDICE OF ALL KINDS MEAN A LIFE OF FEAR FOR THE VICTIMS OF PREJUDICE. DO WHAT YOU CAN TO ELIMINATE IT!

One of our two-page posters reads as follows:
Cover: "Prejudice is being down on something you are not up on!"
Inside: "There can be no prejudice when ignorance is exchanged for empathy!"

In other words, if we could actually change places with

AIDS - Now, One in 250 Americans has the HIV Virus

Acquired Immunodeficiency Syndrome (AIDS) was first discovered in 1981. The disease was originally called Gay-Related Immune Deficiency (GRID), but as researchers became aware that not only homosexual persons were getting sick, the name was changed in 1983.

The disease causes the body's immune system, which fights off disease, to malfunction, leaving the body vulnerable to any number of infections. It is these diseases which ultimately cause sickness and death.

Unfortunately, as this poster goes to press there is no known cure, but research continues and progress is being made.

AIDS is caused by a virus, the Human Immunodeficiency Virus, (HIV). It is transmitted through four body fluids: blood, semen, vaginal fluids, and breast milk. These fluids transmit the virus only if they enter the bloodstream of the person with whom contact is being made.

There are many who still believe all kinds of rumors relevant to contracting this disease. The fact is there are only two possibilities:

1. Sexual activity, including oral, anal, or vaginal intercourse, with someone who is HIV positive, during which HIV in any of the fluids mentioned enters the bloodstream of the non-infected person.
2. Any activity through which HIV-infected blood directly enters the bloodstream of the non-infected person, such as a blood transfusion, or the sharing of hypodermic needles. Mother-to-child HIV transmission is possible both through the birth process and through breast feeding.

Once the Human Immunodeficiency Virus enters the body it invades certain cells in the immune system. Unique to this disease, however, is the fact these infected cells remain dormant for months and even 10 years and longer.

AIDS usually follows a developing state referred to as HIV-positive symptomatic, in which the infected person begins to have flu-like symptoms, including swollen glands, fever, weight loss, diarrhea, and fatigue.

A diagnosis of AIDS is made when a person develops one or more opportunistic diseases, illnesses that overwhelm the weakened immune system.

If you have the slightest doubt about a person with whom you intend to have sex, forget about having sex. Even having a recent blood test is not sufficient. In fact, a window period of up to 6 months exists between the time a person becomes infected with HIV, and the body produces sufficient antibodies to test positive. During this period an infected person can infect others, but will test negative for HIV.

For more information on sexually transmitted diseases, call The National STD Hotline - **1-800-227-8922**. For more information on HIV/AIDS, call the National AIDS Hotline at **1-800-342-AIDS**.

Progressive Publications 1996.

To receive a poster catalog call (352) 382-1452   No. 066

another, living his or her life, we would not be inclined to so quickly condemn.

Having grown up as a Catholic, living first with the nuns, then with the Jesuits in High School and College, I was taught to believe that homosexuals were to be despised for they were sinners and as such deserving of the wrath of civilized society.

So I did my share of gay-bashing and often told jokes about them when I was on the road as a stand-up comic.

Then one day, because of my own curiosity, I went to the library to find some reading material on the subject. I found none. I got the bright idea, that if this is such a controversial subject our library won't even house books on the topic, I better write one!

Something was bugging me, ... if homosexuality is a matter of choice, why in the world would so many people choose this lifestyle, knowing they are going to be ridiculed, physically abused, and even killed for doing so? It didn't make any sense.

Now I never did write a book on the subject, but I did write copy for a pamphlet and it appears on the following pages. I present it here as I firmly believe that to counter prejudice, we must walk in the other man's shoes.

UNDERSTANDING HOMOSEXUALITY

Evidence continues to surface which confirms that homo-sexuality is the direct result of genetic composition, and yet many continue to shout from the pulpit that homosexuality is unnatural, biblically condemned, and a lifestyle lived by sinners.

How much chemistry affects behavior continues to be revealed each year. As research of scientists advances it seems clear that biology is the basis for homosexuality, ... that personal preference has no bearing on one's sexual orientation.

Now if you were to ask many who claim to be Christians to accept these revelations most would reply that they can't for to do so would be against their religion. Chances are they have accepted the position of their church which has gone on unchallenged for years. Perhaps it is time to think again.

Actually, the Bible says nothing about homosexuality relevant to orientation, nor does the Bible say anything about homosexual persons. The Biblical writers assumed everyone was what we term *heterosexual,* just as they assumed the sun revolved around the earth.

Assumptions can be dangerous slander if allowed to spread. Many might determine that a man in his thirties who associates solely with men, who never has gone out on a date with a woman, must obviously be gay? Right? Not necessarily, for if this were so then many would have to conclude that Jesus Christ was homosexual.

Biblical scholars have said that 10% of what appears in the Bible may be accurate, but they also disagree on what 10% may be factual.

Now there is not reference in the New Testament about homosexual activity by Jesus or anyone else in the four gospels, so we can attribute all Biblical condemnation to what appears in the Old Testament.

In Leviticus (18:22 and 20:13) it says "Males are not to lie with males." As Jews in those days felt homosexuality was a practice characteristic of the Canaanites and the Egyptians, it was culturally demeaning for a Jew to act in a similar fashion. The reason for the statement is therefore in question. Other pagan practices which the book of Leviticus condemned with equal authority were the eating of rabbit, pork, oysters, shrimp, lobster, and rare steak.

To loosely interpret the words in Leviticus or perhaps references made by Paul, to form opinions which justify condemnation of homosexuals, is to ignore the words of Christ himself who advocated "love of God and love of your neighbor as yourself."

Harvard graduate John Boswell did a ten year long study of this subject prior to publishing the book, "Christianity, Social Tolerance, and Homosexuality. His conclusion: that nothing in Christian scripture censures homosexuality.

Prior to publishing a book on sexual orientation, research by personnel at Progressive Publications included joining Gay organizations with the intention of surveying members. Over 100 individuals were asked if they made a conscious decision to be gay. None said they did. In fact, many said: "Are you kidding?, why would I choose an orientation which alienates me from society and invites everyone who despises gays to abuse me?"

Although the book was never written, the research gave ample logic to the argument that *choice* is not an option in regard to sexual orientation.

Much more convincing than this hearsay evidence, however, is the research recently completed by Dr. Dean Hamer. In his new book, *The Science of Desire* he confirms certain facts: "Personality characteristics are influenced by genes which are passed from generation to generation." and "There is such a thing as a gay gene and it does run in families."

It is obvious then that a person born as a homosexual has no more chance of determining his sexual orientation, than any man has of determining the color of his skin or such personality characteristics as being aggressive or not.

As each of us on this planet is different in looks, so it is that we are different biologically. No doubt in years to come we will learn more about genetic alteration before birth and chemical alternatives to correct undesirable characteristics for the living. Until then we have ample evidence which suggests we should be both understanding and tolerant.

"There but for the grace of God go I."

Today, much is said that depicts homosexual lifestyles as being devoid of family values, and yet it is not these members of our society who create unwanted pregnancies and abortions.

Can not homosexuals live as directed by the advice of Christ? Of course. And who among us is so righteous that he or she can say "I am right and all who think otherwise are unquestionably wrong."

Those parents of homosexuals who read this can take heart. It was not something you did or didn't do in child rearing which caused your son or daughter to be gay.

Yes, it was passed on through your genes, but so were many of the characteristics you see in them. Take pride, and for heavens sake take down any fences which went up after your sons or daughters came out of the closet.

Extend your hand if you have been declining to do so and offer your understanding and your everlasting love.

Your reward for doing so will be receiving the love you have been denying yourself.

Even though you might find it difficult to approve a relationship between two people of the same sex, consider what it would be like if someone told you that further contact with members of the opposite sex would not be allowed.

If in fact, people are born with characteristics which we dislike, do any of us have the right to oppose them?, openly criticize them?, physically abuse them? Absolutely not!

This information is printed in a pamphlet and is available through Progressive Publications. To receive a free copy, send your request along with a stamped self addressed envelope to: Progressive Publications
P.O. Box 4016
Homosassa Springs, FL 34447

4. WE MUST DO WHAT WE CAN TO GET ACROSS THE IDEA THAT IT IS NOT NECESSARY TO LIVE BY TRIAL AND ERROR, THAT THE WISE MAN LEARNS FROM THE MISTAKES OF OTHERS.

So many young people turn a deaf ear to advice if it is offered by someone over 25. Kind of reminds me of the two strangers meeting in a store for the first time:

*Learn from the mistakes of others —
you can never live
long enough to make
them all yourself.*

Clerk: "Have a nice day!"
Customer: "Don't you tell me what to do!"

A box containing a few thousand letters from prisoners sits in the corner of my office. It is the result of a book written a few years ago titled: *From Prison To Prosperity.* In this book we explore the possibility of self-employment for ex-convicts and how it can be accomplished with little or no money to start.

After finding out how few prisons had money for books of this type, a management decision was made to give the book away to all prisoners who wrote a letter requesting it. We informed the Correctional Education Association of this decision and letters started coming in shortly thereafter. That was three years ago and the letters are still coming despite the fact the book is out of print.

Each letter is a fascinating story of "knowing it all" when in reality, ... "I knew nothing, and wouldn't listen to anyone!"

Too bad they had to lose years out of their lives before they became smart enough to say, "I'm ready to learn from the mistakes of others."

The poster on this subject is one that should put a smile on anyone's face. Make copies on your copy machine then pass them out to those who are maintaining a "my way is the only way" attitude.

5. BE ALERT TO THE INDICATIONS A STUDENT MAY ATTEMPT SUICIDE AND BE PREPARED TO PROVIDE HOPE.

Every year increasing numbers of U.S. citizens take their own lives, now about 30,000. Among this number are many young people. In fact according to the National Center for Health Statistics, over the last ten years the number of suicides in the 15 to 24 year old age group have shown alarming increases.

The reasons one might want to die are many. They include intense feelings of depression, loneliness, helplessness, and a complete lack of self-esteem. These all contribute to a common characteristic among candidates for suicide, ... the total absence of hope.

Teen pregnancies are often the reason both boys and girls attempt suicide. They believe the consequences of their actions are impossible to resolve. As an educator, you must provide other answers.

Incidentally, you should know that although seven girls attempt suicide for every boy that does, more boys actually kill themselves than do girls.

Be on the alert for clues which might indicate a student might seriously attempt suicide. If you either know someone or hear of someone talking about taking their own life, assume he or she is serious.

Here are some common indications:

- CHANGES IN PERSONALITY. The person shows an increasing tendency to withdraw, be pensive, spend more time alone.

- CHANGES IN BEHAVIOR. The person loses weight, says "I'm not hungry", indicates no sexual desire.

- THREATENS TO "TAKE A LONG TRIP", "END IT ALL", ETC. Take these comments seriously. They are often cries for help. If no one hears, they can also be accurate predictions.

- CHANGES IN STUDY HABITS. Declines an interest in school subjects or in hobbies or work once enjoyed.

- PREPARATIONS FOR DEATH ARE MADE. The person acquires a gun, a rope, pills, poison, etc. The person makes out a will, writes a letter, gives personal belongings away.

Knowing the above, if you should have any suspicion about a student needing help, take it upon yourself to indicate your desire to be of assistance.

A. Tell the person you care about them and that you are there to help them at any time.

B. Ask concerned questions, but spend as much time as you can listening.

C. Explain that with help and support and the passage of time, life will change for the better. "Good times" will come again and you will help provide a new view of the future.

If you haven't done so already make copies of the poem which appears on page 71 and distribute them to those who seem down. The message of this work is simply that we must forget about the past and concentrate on all the great happy times which we have the power to make happen.

- Stay in close touch until you see the risk has passed.

D. HERE ARE SOME *DO's & DON'Ts* YOU SHOULD KNOW

- Don't try to use psychology by challenging the person to "Go ahead and try it!" Leave the psychology up to professionals. Your biggest job is to get this person to see a professional.

- Don't analyze the person's motives, for example, "You just feel bad because ..." Again, leave this type of conjecture up to the professionals, regardless of how sure you are that you know the answers.

- Don't argue with the person or try to reason with him or her. There is a very real possibility you could make matters worse and actually be the cause of a suicide attempt.

E. HERE ARE SOME SUGGESTIONS YOU MIGHT TRY

- Get the person involved in a new project, sport, avocation, hobby. Try to give the person a sound reason to live.

- Escort the person to the library. Chances are that there are books available which will detail the experiences of those who had similar problems.

- Suggest therapy. Look up the names of those professionals who might help. Share your findings with the person you are trying to assist.

- Keep the individual busy if at all possible. Assist with creating new plans for the future.

Some years ago, at a time in my life when I really felt I had more problems than I could handle, I had the great good fortune to meet Norman Vincent Peale. When I told him of my "problems" he said "Well aren't you lucky."

"What?", I managed to utter, "Why am I lucky?" He explained, and I have never since forgotten this bit of wisdom.

"Living life creates problems." "Now, you can shut yourself away in a closet and avoid these problems, but is that living?" "If in fact you have twice as many problems as the next guy just indicates that you are probably doing twice as much living." "Rejoice!, you are indeed a fortunate person."

5. ALL STUDENTS WHO EXPERIENCE PHYSICAL AND/OR EMOTIONAL PAIN LIVE WITH FEAR WHICH KEEPS THEM FROM FOCUSING ON THEIR PRIMARY OBJECTIVES. THIS IS THE CAUSE OF MANY DROP-OUTS.

If your school is like most, the phrase "WE CARE" probably appears somewhere in your collateral materials. Of course if you are like most schools, the person who inserted that catchy phrase is sitting across town somewhere at an agency whose job it is to make up catchy phrases.

Unfortunately, most schools only pay lip service to this statement.

If you and your associates truly want to give meaning to this phrase, then all of you must assist your counselors by actually providing help rather than merely suggesting to a student that he or she should get help.

You might start by knowing every professional in town who might be of assistance to your students. Then set up a *SCHOOL HELP REFERENCE GUIDE* for everyone to use. This "GUIDE" should include but never be restricted to the following:

- ALCOHOLICS ANONYMOUS. Where they are. Who heads the program. Name of contact for personal referrals. Days and times of meetings.

- ALYNON. (For the spouses of alcoholics)

- CENTERS FOR THE VICTIMS OF ABUSE. Names of those who will work with your students.

- HELP FOR THOSE GETTING DIVORCED. Names of attorneys students can consult at no cost. Names of marriage counselors students can consult at no cost. Names of support groups.

- CHILD CARE. All alternatives near your school, licensed and unlicensed. Costs, names of principals and their educational backgrounds, references of former students, meals, and all other related data.

- FREE LEGAL ADVICE. Where. Who. Specialties in law.

- FREE OR LOW COST DENTAL CARE. Where. Who. Hours.

- FREE OR LOW COST MEDICAL CARE. Where. Who. Hours. Specialties.

- FREE CLOTHING STORES OR LOW COST SECOND HAND STORES. Where. Who. Hours.

- FREE OR LOW COST PSYCHOLOGICAL CARE. Who. Where. Hours.

- COUNSELING FOR HOMOSEXUALS. Who. Where. Hours.

- COUNSELING FOR THOSE WITH SEXUALLY TRANSMITTED DISEASES INCLUDING THE HIV VIRUS. Where. Who. Hours.

- DRUG REHABILITATION CENTERS. Where. Who. Hours.

- TRANSPORTATION SOLUTIONS. Names of students who will participate in driving pools. Low cost means.

Now please understand the difference in the level of involvement. The person who truly cares will take the student by the hand, escort him or her to their car, drive him or her to the source of the assistance needed, introduce him or her to the contacts there, and drive him or her back to your school at the conclusion of the session.

This is a far cry from handing a student a piece of paper with a name and address on it and saying "see you later." With that kind of "caring", later could be a matter of years and very often never.

7. CONSIDER BEING INSTRUMENTAL IN SETTING UP A SEPARATE NON-PROFIT CORPORATION AT YOUR SCHOOL WHICH WILL PROVIDE EMERGENCY

FUNDS FOR ALL STUDENTS WITH UNUSUAL
NEEDS.

At a school I ran in California, it was common to hear
excuses for absence which included "I ripped the only
pair of jeans I own", "I just didn't have bus fare", "Even
if I could have found enough money to buy a used tire,
I would have been here." etc., etc.

This fund, once established, could provide loans, not
gifts, to provide temporary help for all student needs.
All those receiving assistance would understand that
they have an obligation to repay the loan at their first
opportunity even though no date for repayment or an
interest charge is made part of the loan.

To fund this corporation, consider having an annual
raffle if this is legal in your state.

Also keep administrative costs of the fund at a minimum
by asking for faculty and student volunteers to oversee
the program. To avoid any possibility of embezzlement
always make sure that multiple signatures are required
to validate each check.

Even though it may seem far-fetched to believe that a
student may drop out because he or she lacks "the bus
fare for the rest of the week", you can be sure it has
happened more than once. Make sure it never happens
at your school from this day on. Start a fund.

8. TEACH YOUR STUDENTS HOW TO SOLVE
PROBLEMS.

At various times in our lives, we all experience problems
we would very much like to live without.

THE DIFFERENCE BETWEEN A PROBLEM FINDER AND A PROBLEM SOLVER

THE PROBLEM FINDER

Problem Finders are easy to find. They are everywhere. They look like everyone else, however, they are more readily identified by sound. They say such things as, "somebody should do something about that," or "the rules are stupid," or "my boss is a jerk." The tone of their voice is also denotable. They whine, they cry, they shout, and seldom if ever consider that they possibly could be the cause of the problem. As such, they live with self-sympathy and a vehemently defensive attitude. They are never wrong, consequently, they find it impossible to apologize. They can't wait to spread slander, love to belittle others, and can hardly let an hour go by without complaining about someone or something.

Generally speaking, you can locate them in jobs which require little thought, little creativity, little responsibility, and no leadership ability. That is, if you can find them working at all. They are despised by employers, and at best, tolerated by conscientious co-workers, family members and would-be friends.

Problem finders are negative thinkers and, as such, chronic pessimists. They are depressing to be around and as a result have few friends. Their smiles are few and far between. They can't seem to smell the roses along the way, and simply aren't capable of being happy. They live with selfish motives in a lonely world.

If you know such persons, befriend them, be honest, be frank. Make them aware of the benefits of change. It can occur. Thank God, IT CAN OCCUR.

THE PROBLEM SOLVER

These persons are ninety times more difficult to find than the Problem Finders, but are still easily recognized by sight and sound. They find smiling comes easy and they project an image of self-confidence. Their immediate response to any problem, whether personally involved or not, is "What can I do to find a solution?"

Problems to them aren't something to simply complain about, procrastinate with or ignore altogether. Problems are challenges, opportunities to prove one's value when solved. Problem Solvers realize that with each solution found they become more valuable as leaders, as benefactors and as masters of their own destinies. They are wise enough to know they, too, will make mistakes, but unhesitatingly proceed to make decisions until the correct one is made.

Problem Solvers are positive thinkers, and as such, eternal optimists. They understand the futility of complaints, criticism, slander and living in the past. They also understand the promise for fulfilment which comes with goal setting, imagination and persistence.

Problem Solvers are leaders and do-ers. Always active, never bored and forever looking for new horizons. As such, they are sought after by more intelligent employers and bask in the luxury of good fortune. They are respected, admired and capable of greater love as they can see the good in the worst of men.

If you know such persons, stay close, and emulate their actions. You will grow in the greatness and never experience the pains of loneliness or poverty.

rogressive Publications © Copyright 1996.   To receive a poster catalog call (352) 382-1452   No. 036

Trying hard not to acknowledge the problem, however, thinking "maybe it will go away", seldom works.

A wise man once offered me the "Greatest Problem Solving Technique" known to mankind. I was skeptical at the time, but since then have learned to appreciate the wisdom of this advice. The entire technique is just three short words: MAKE A DECISION.

Once you make a decision to effect a change, your problem will no longer stay the same. Sometimes you find a solution. Sometimes you succeed in making the problem worse, but one thing is sure, the original problem no longer exists. Keep making decisions and sooner or later you will be the victor.

Having a positive attitude when attacking a problem is almost essential, so from this minute on view no quandry as a problem. From now on all problems are to be considered challenges to your ability. Solutions are not only going to be possible, but they are inevitable certainties.

Now as I have already brought up the name of Norman Peale, you probably know I am an active exponent of his work. Get a copy of *The Power of Positive Thinking* when you can and thereafter loan it to students who can benefit from reading it.

Also make copies of the poster which appears on the preceding page and keep them handy to pass out to the moaners and groaners you come across. You'll see more doing, less complaining.

By saving people from living with everlasting problems, you will positively prevent drop-outs.

9. USE FEAR TO SCHOOL STUDENTS ON THE EFFECTS OF MARIJUANA AND DRUGS AVAILABLE ON THE STREET.

Early in this book we included a poster titled *Sing Your Own Song*. It is our answer to those who feel a need to give in to temptation in order to be included in a group.

Peer pressure is indeed a problem, mostly because those who are luring the Pinocchios of the world are doing so with lies, misinformation and grand imaginary promises.

So you won't find any drug dealers who take pride in their integrity and honest sales pitches, and yet thousands buy their spiel every day.

Whether you are in school administration or teach biology, psychology, or auto mechanics, please take a few minutes of your class time to provide reliable information about marijuana and drugs.

Make copies of the information provided in the posters on the following two pages, distribute it, and hold discussions with students. If you have students who were previously addicted but are now clean, ask them to share their experience with their classmates.

No mind altering drugs can be taken without causing side effects. Take it upon yourself to get this message across.

FACTS ABOUT
MARIJUANA

- In 1995, 42 percent of high school seniors said they have smoked marijuana. 34 percent of 10th graders said they had smoked marijuana. 20 percent of 8th graders said they had smoked marijuana.

- Of all those who have tried marijuana, the average age of their first exposure to this drug was 13.5 years.

- The rise in marijuana use over the last three years has been attributed to far fewer messages to teens detailing anti-drug reasoning. Wayne Roques, Drug Enforcement Administrator said: "Whenever the perception of risk goes down, use goes up. That's exactly what has happened."

- Contrary to stereotypes, marijuana use is heaviest among white males and females. According to the Center on Addiction and Substance Abuse, the percent of seniors who used this drug in the previous 12 months is as follows: (Years 1985-1989)

WHITE MALES	40.2 %
BLACK MALES	29.8 %
WHITE FEMALES	36.0 %
BLACK FEMALES	18.4 %

- According to the National Institute of Drug Abuse, continuing use of marijuana inevitably affects the brain and leads to impaired short term memory, impaired perception, impaired judgement and noticeable reductions in abilities related to motor skills.

- "The potency of the marijuana distributed today is far stronger than the "pot" passed around on college campuses back in the sixties" says DEA agents. The strength is determined by measuring the THC (Delta-9-Tetrahydrocannabinol, a psychoactive chemical). According to Mahmoud Elsohly, a research chemist at the University of Mississippi, and this country's leading expert on the potency of marijuana, the marijuana being used today can be as much as 28 times stronger than the drug used in the sixties.

- Although you may not realize it yourself, continual use of marijuana will change your behavior. Among the most common signs are:

Your friends will sense you are different, may start to avoid you.

You will lack interest in activities you used to consider to be interesting, fun, or pleasurable.

You will sleep far less than you used to.

Your eating habits will change, items you once enjoyed will no longer taste the same.

You will be more defensive and argumentative with both your parents and friends.

You will experience increasing signs of ill-health, ... nausea, headaches, bloodshot eyes, slurred speech, runny nose, hangovers.

Your grades will drop. You'll experience an increased number of problems with teachers and school personnel.

Source: Gannett News Service.

- A survey conducted by Pride, an Atlanta based drug education and prevention group, showed students who used marijuana as infrequently as once a year, were six times more likely to threaten another student, nine times more likely to get into trouble with the police, and nine times more likely to carry a gun.

- FOR MORE INFORMATION ON MARIJUANA USE CALL OR WRITE:

Monitoring the Future Study
University of Michigan
Ann Arbor, MI 48109

The National Institute on Drug Abuse
1-800-729-6686

Progressive Publications© Copyright 1996.

DRUGS ON THE STREET

These are the most widely abused drugs, their effects and hazards. Experts note that most abusers, including problem drinkers, use more than one drug; and when combined, these substances can have dangerously unpredictable effects. Legally prescribed narcotics and tranquillizers are also widely abused, especially in combination with alcohol.

ALCOHOL

Depressant. Physically addictive. The oldest, most widely used and abused drug. Consumption under the age of 21 illegal in Virginia and most other states, but underage use widespread; driving under influence and public drunkenness are crimes. Excessive drinking impairs senses, speech, reflexes and coordination. Problem drinking or addiction (alcoholism) intensifies emotional problems and causes liver and cardiovascular diseases. Some pharmaceutical treatments, but self-help therapy programs such as Alcoholics Anonymous more common. Alcoholics who do not seek treatment and fail to practice lifetime abstinence usually relapse into addictive use.

HEROIN Dope, diesel, boy

Depressant. Physically addictive. Synthetic developed from morphine, derived from opium. Mixed for street sale with fillers such as quinine or milk sugar. Traditionally injected, but in purer form can be snorted or smoked. Dulls senses and appetite, produces feeling of well-being and semiconscious state ("nod"). Effects typically last three to six hours. Intravenous users risk HIV infection and AIDS. Overdose can produce seizures, cardiac arrest, coma, death. Heroin addicts also may use medicinal opiates, prescribed as painkillers and cough suppressants. Methadone and other pharmaceutical opiates widely used in maintenance treatment for withdrawal. Relapses common.

COCAINE Coke, rock, girl

Stimulant. Physically or psychologically addictive (experts differ). Derived from the coca plant. Once used as antidepressant and anesthetic. "Cut" with various fillers for street sale. Powdered form is snorted and rubbed in gums; crystallized crack cocaine is smoked; or melted and injected, sometimes in combination with heroin ("speedball"). Reduces appetite, produces euphoric state, aggressiveness in some cases; some users consider it an aphrodisiac. In powdered form, effects last one to two hours; crack effects more intense with duration of as little as five minutes. Cyclical ("binge") use common. Overdose can cause cardiac arrest, coma, death. Withdrawal accompanied by depression, lethargy, sleep disorders. Therapy, but no accepted medicinal treatment for withdrawal. Relapses common, especially among crack users.

AMPHETAMINES Speed, crank

Stimulants. Physically addictive. Once prescribed as diet pills and to treat narcolepsy; Ritalin used to treat hyperactivity. Known as "speed" or "crank," amphetamines (swallowed) and methamphetamines (injected) reduce appetite, produce energetic, nervous state, paranoia and suicidal tendencies in some cases. Effects last two or four hours. Cyclical use similar to that of cocaine. Withdrawal similar to post-cocaine "crash," but more dangerous.

BARBITURATES Downers

Depressants. Physically addictive. Used medicinally as tranquillizers and sleeping pills. Produce relaxed state, elation in some cases. Distort time perception and may cause memory lapses. Extremely dangerous in combination with alcohol or other depressants; overdose can produce coma or death. Withdrawal can produce seizures, delirium, hallucinations. Nonbarbiturate tranquillizers, more commonly prescribed today, can have similar effects if misused.

MARIJUANA Bud, blunt, pot

Hallucinogen. Traditionally thought nonaddictive, but recent research suggests at least phychological addiction. Dried leaves and flowers of hemp plant; hashish is resin from flowers of plant. The most widely used illegal drug, often used in combination with other drugs. Smoked or eaten. Produces various "highs," from euphoric to lethargic; hunger, impaired coordination and short term memory loss are common side effects. Effects last two to four hours. High tar content damages lungs when smoked. Withdrawal generally "cold turkey" with minor symptoms. Not widely treated unless marijuana used in combination with more serious drugs such as heroin or cocaine.

OTHER HALLUCINOGENS

Most popular are LSD and PCP. Psychologically addictive. LSD synthesized from grain fungus, once used in psychiatric research and to treat alcoholism, but now medically discredited. Eaten. Produces euphoric and "out-of-body" states, hallucinations and other sensory distortions. Mescaline (peyote) has similar effects. PCP ("angel dust") developed as animal tranquillizer. Sprinkled on marijuana or parsley and smoked or eaten. Depresses or stimulates, depending on dosage. Overdose produces disorientation, delusions, seizures. Can cause anxiety, paranoia or other mental problems if used repeatedly. Duration of effects varies; LSD "trip" can last eight to 10 hours. "Crash" withdrawal; "flashback" after effects not uncommon with LSD.

INHALANTS

Toxic substances, including glue, gasoline, solvents, insecticides and other aerosol sprays. Addictive qualities debated. Sniffed. Many are highly flammable. Nitrous oxide (laughing gas), used in aerosols and as anesthetic, is nonflammable. Produce varying states of intoxication, often disorientation; can induce coma. Intense, short term effects.

SOURCES: U.S. Department of Justice; "Overview of Substance Abuse" by Peter Coleman, M.D. (Primary Care, March 1993); "The Clinical Treatment of Substance Abuse" by Leon Brill (The Free Press)

CHAPTER 9

GETTING STUDENTS TO SET SPECIFIC CAREER AND EMPLOYMENT OBJECTIVES AS SOON AS POSSIBLE AFTER ARRIVING ON CAMPUS

There are many educators who still advocate a liberal arts education, and for those who are born with silver spoons in their mouths, this still may be sound advice.

With the cost of post-secondary education skyrocketing, however, not having specific career and employment goals in mind can lead procrastinators to an awesome mountain of debt.

If any student attending a post-secondary school feels sure that his or her institution is the best means through which he or she can achieve both a career objective as well as a specific employment objective, that student will never drop out.

Make sense? Of course! So if we are to eliminate drop-outs, the best possible assistance we can provide to our students is showing them how to establish these goals.

For years School Placement Departments have been very busy places as graduation nears.

In the meantime if we stopped the average student on campus and asked: What are you going to do after you graduate, most would say, "Well, I hope to get a job ..... etc." Where? Who knows!

"Choose a job you love, and you will never have to work a day in your life."

Confucius

To make this possible, follow these steps ...

● Set goals immediately to find both the career that is right for you and then a very specific employment position where you can best pursue your career.

● Assuming you have already chosen a career and the school which can best help you achieve expertise in your field, set objectives to be the "Best that you can be!" In other words just don't settle for passing grades, ... spend your school hours wisely. While others are in the student lounge discussing "General Hospital," you are spending your time developing your skills.

● Starting today, start your search for that one employer for whom you would most like to work. Go to conventions, ask everyone you meet, who is employed in "your career," if they are happily employed. If so, note where they work, what benefits they have, what the philosophy of the company is, if employees are treated as individuals or numbers, if management considers their employees to be their most important asset.

● If you like what you hear, make a point of going to visit all prospective employers. Talk to everyone you meet, from the janitor on up. Ask, "How do you like working here?" Listen! Keep in mind that if the janitor is treated with respect, chances are you have found an employer who truly cares about others. Try to find out who would be your immediate supervisor if you were to be hired there, and who would have the responsibility of giving the final OK before you would be hired.

● Call these V.I.P.s, ask if you can have five minutes of their time to ask about their company. Explain that you are a student attending _____ school, but that you really want to work for this company some day, and want to know how you can best prepare yourself to be hired.

● If you are right in your assessment of the company, chances are the person you are contacting will grant you an interview. When you meet, be very thorough in recording all the hints given to you about how to get hired there. Before you leave you should have ample information to prepare a "tailor made" resume.

Finding your "Ideal Job," where it's a joy to come to work each day, doesn't often just happen because you "got lucky." You must make it happen with foresight and hard work. Do it!

Keep this in mind: The more students you have wandering your campus waiting for the *Job Fairy* to wave her magic wand and provide them with divine guidance, the more drop-outs you will have.

So it is logical to do everything you can to assist every student to choose a career and then find the single-best employer in the entire world for whom they would most like to work.

Placement Departments should be their busiest as students first arrive on campus.

Let's consider an example:

Mary Ann decides that she wants to be a secretary. She enrolls at the school of her choice and attends orientation.

Now, a funny thing happens: Instead of leaving the door open to extraordinary accomplishment, the administrator says: In order to graduate, you must type 55 words a minute and do at least this, that, and a little of the other thing!

So Mary Ann is now provided with objectives she must meet to get a diploma. Objectives that will at best provide her with average skills.

Is it any wonder the average graduate at the average Business School graduates with a typing average around 55 words per minute?

And this scenario isn't exclusive to those who want to be secretaries, the same blunder is often made with all students. They are told up front how little they need do to graduate, rather than how much better employed they might be if they get better grades.

So what have we done? Something stupid, that's what ! We took away the visual goal of being a secretary, and replaced it with a paper reward called a diploma.

Now if we could take this piece of paper down to a cashier someplace and redeem it for X amount of dollars or a job paying specific dollars, our guidance might be understandable, but as this is not so, this type of advice is actually counter-productive.

How can we provide goals which will really pay off? Simple, we get all our students out looking for the employer for whom they would most like to work, ... as soon as possible.

After going to conventions, and asking every secretary in town if they work for an employer they like, Mary Ann finds the employer for whom she would most like to work. We then encourage her to call up the V.I.P. heading the Department where she would like to work, and ask him or her for 10 minutes of their time for an "Informational Interview."

If she is right in her assumption that the employer is a good one, the V.I.P. will probably grant her request for an interview. Why? Because good employers understand the value of considering their employees to be their most important asset.

If the V.I.P. says, "Go away, you bother me!", Mary Ann has also found out something valuable, that maybe this isn't the place she wants to work.

At the interview, Mary Ann then says something like this: "Mr. Jones, I really want to work here some day." "So, I want you to tell me what qualifcations you would suggest I

143

have to get employed." I am just starting school over at X College and you can help me design my classes."

The V.I.P. then might say something like this: "Well, as you have already found out that this is a very desirable place to work, you can understand that we have more applicants for every opening than most places. So if you really want to work here some day, I would suggest that you type at least 85 words per minute, know computers thoroughly, and be familiar with Blah!, Blah! and Blah!"

Now Mary Ann goes back to her school with very specific goals in mind and is no longer influenced by the mediocre objectives the school sets as minimums.

While the other students are sitting in the student lounge every morning discussing what occurred on General Hospital the day before, Mary Ann is in the typing room gaining speed.

Success has often been described as "the progressive realization of a worthy goal." You can make your students immediately successful as soon as you assist them to establish very specific employment goals.

And once they have, they will not drop out. You can bet on it.

CHAPTER 10

HOW TO ESTABLISH MORE EFFICIENT PLACEMENT ASSISTANCE AT POSTSECONDARY SCHOOLS, ... A MUST IF YOU INTEND TO IMPLEMENT AND MAINTAIN AN EFFECTIVE PLAN OF STUDENT RETENTION !

The ideas listed below are in no particular order nor are all of them applicable at all schools. Any one of them, however, might trigger a new concept or procedure you can adapt for your use.

1. AT THE TIME OF ENROLLMENT, MAKE SURE EVERY NEW STUDENT KNOWS THAT PARTICIPATION IN PLACEMENT CLASSES IS MANDATORY UNLESS THE STUDENT SIGNS A WAIVER OF PLACEMENT FORM RELINQUISHING SCHOOL PLACEMENT ASSISTANCE.

   When answering the obvious question, "Why?", let it be known that the *Image* of any school is determined by the success of its graduates. And mastering the "science" of getting a job is often the instrumental key which leads to superior placement.

   Please understand this: Although the average student sincerely believes he or she knows how to get a job, they know very little. Their experience for the most part has been fast food. In reality, they don't have a clue what it is going to be like to compete for a superior job.

Now that you know this, it is your responsibility to pass on the idea that "job-getting skills" must be developed, that "getting lucky", happens mostly in the movies.

2. AT ORIENTATION, MAKE SURE ALL STUDENTS KNOW THEY WILL HAVE TO DEVOTE NO LESS THAN ONE HOUR PER WEEK TO THEIR "JOB PLACEMENT CLASSES."

Subjects can include, but should not be restricted to, the following:

A) That you expect your graduates to get no less than $1.20 more per hour than the average hourly starting wage for the occupation being entered.

   At this session, show how this hourly wage will amount to $48.00 per week, $2,440.00 per year, and if invested at 10%, accumulate a retirement fund after 40 years of $1,168,444.00.

B) The mastermind concept as described in "Think & Grow Rich" by Napoleon Hill.

C) Understanding the *Rule of 72*.

D) Understand the concept, *Research Before Resumes.*

E) The difference a *MUST DO TODAY* list can make in ultimately finding the "Ideal Job."

F) Understand how to research prospective employers.

G) How to set up appointments to get *Informational Interviews.*

H) Use of the telephone to find the right people to contact, and then how to talk to them to set up an interview.

I) How to *Dress For Success.*

J) How *Body Language* during the interview can help you get the job or cost you the job.

K) The *Psychology of Touching.*

L) How to talk clearly and with personality. (This session should include role-playing)

M) The Resume.

N) The Cover Letter.

O) Gaining Self Esteem (Introduce audio and video tapes.)

P) Checklist of items to cover before going on a job interview. (See poster on the next page, make reduced copies, distribute them for this session.)

Q) How to sell yourself in an interview.

R) What to do after the interview if you really want the job.

S) How to respond to illegal questions often asked in an interview.

T) How to fill out a job application and why it is important that you take a copy of it with you when you go on a job interview.

Job Interview Preparation Checklist

A chain is only as strong as its weakest link. Your plan to get hired is similar. Just one weak aspect can overshadow all your strong points. One inadvertent slip-of-the-tongue and you've blown it! One admission of ignorance and it's "back to the drawing board." One "I don't know" and it's return to square one time.

Be ready or stay home!

The entire purpose of the step-by-step procedure is to make sure you are organized - more organized than any of your competition. If you have followed directions, you undoubtedly are, but as a final act before leaving for the interview, let's make sure.

Go over the following checklist. Make a mental "✓" in the boxes in the right-hand column if you can answer yes.

1. I know how to dress and have picked out the clothes I know will be viewed as acceptable. ☐

2. I know the means of transportation I am going to use to get to the interview. ☐

3. If I am driving a car, I know it is running well and I have checked the tires, the oil and the gas. ☐

4. I Know the route I am going to travel and I know what time I must leave in order to get there, at least, fifteen (15) minutes early. ☐

5. I know where I can park and I have money to park. ☐

6. I know the name of the receptionist and/or the name of the secretary of the person who will conduct the interview. ☐

7. I know the name and the correct title of the person(s) who will hold the interview, and I know a great deal about their personality and background. ☐

8. I know the name of the Department Head who will play a role in the hiring decision, and I have researched background and personality. ☐

9. I know who owns the company (names, titles, etc.). If a corporation, I know the names of the officers and the Board Members, and a few facts on all of them. ☐

10. I will take a briefcase or attache case with me to the interview, and have it packed with: a) an application (already filled out), b) additional copies of my resume (only if already sent), c) samples of my work, d) additional letters of reference or communication, e) a notebook to record any dates, names, pertinent facts, etc., that I can use later in follow-up letters, and f) my purse (if a woman). ☐

11. I know a great deal about the company, products or services, policies, procedures, profits, etc. ☐

12. I have studied the questions I will most likely be asked and I am prepared to answer them. ☐

13. I feel I know the type of employee the average employer wants to hire and I have prepared statements which should answer their concerns. ☐

14. I know the signals which indicate the company may be interested in hiring me. ☐

15. I know the questions I intend to ask after the company has shown an interest in hiring me. ☐

16. I know to ask a question in return when asked a question that is illegal to ask, or one that I simply would prefer not to answer. ☐

17. I know the salary range and benefits I will ask for after the company has indicated a desire to hire me. ☐

18. I know the specific job I would like to have with this company, and I have studied the job description. ☐

19. I understand how to observe the interviewer's office to look for conversational clues. ☐

20. I know I am to speak up. I know what to say and what not to say. I know how to put expression in my voice. I know when to shut up and be a good listener. ☐

21. I know I am going to shake hands firmly while looking people in the eyes. ☐

22. I know the posture I want to use while standing, walking and sitting. ☐

23. I understand the value of using people's names, but I also know that, when addressing people in responsible positions, it is safe to address people as "Ms.," "Mrs.," or "Mister," regardless of age differences. ☐

24. I have prepared a few one-liners to use if the opportunity presents itself. ☐

25. I know the closing statement I am going to use if I feel I really would like the job. ☐

26. I know the statement I am going to make if I am not sure I want the job. ☐

27. I know how to reject an offer of employment without causing resentment. ☐

28. I realize I must be polite if rejected in the interview and act with class and distinction. ☐

29. If rejected in the interview, I am prepared to tactfully ask "why" by soliciting the help of the Interviewer. ☐

30. I am mentally prepared to sell myself with enthusiasm. I am going to step in the door with a smile on my face, and everyone I meet is going to like me. ☐

I AM READY!

To receive a poster catalog call (352) 382-1452   No. 075

U) Intelligent Appearance. Knowing about cosmetics, haircuts, jewelry, body piercing, tattoos, sun glasses, perfume and cologne, clothing, shoes, etc.

V) Sessions based on different personality characteristics.

W) How to advance on the job after being hired. (See poster with this title on the next page, make reduced copies for distribution, discuss each point.)

3. CONSIDER FORMING JOB SEARCH TEAMS, FROM 3 TO 7 STUDENTS EACH, AS SOON AS POSSIBLE AFTER SCHOOL STARTS.

The members of each team should have similar career and employment objectives.

The members of each team elect a team leader.

The members of each team make a pledge to assist their teammates with any problem whether it is personal or related to their studies. They further pledge to see to it no member of the team drops out of school.

A monitor employed by the school meets with team leaders, supports activities, offers subject matter for weekly meetings, assists with setting up *team* informational interviews, brings in employers to attend team meetings, attends all meetings, offers solutions to problems, celebrates with the team anytime there is a reason to celebrate.

4. MAINTAIN A V.I.P. LIST OF ALL EMPLOYERS IN YOUR CITY OR COUNTY WHO HAVE PREVIOUSLY HIRED YOUR GRADUATES.

12 WAYS TO PROMOTE YOURSELF AFTER FINDING YOUR "IDEAL JOB"

1. From your first day on, show up early. Never be late. Salaries go up as responsibility increases. Those who are chronically late, label themselves irresponsible. And, as such, not suited for supervisory positions.

2. Study the Science of Handling People. This skill, if soundly developed, will result in more advancement opportunities than any subject you have mastered in school. Start with buying a copy of Dale Carnegie's HOW TO WIN FRIENDS AND INFLUENCE PEOPLE. this book has been a best seller for many years and for a good reason. We wholeheartedly recommend it.

3. From your first hour on the new job, write a training manual while you learn. Answer those questions that perplex you in print so that the person who replaces you will be able to adapt more quickly without the pain that accompanies trial and error. Show it to your supervisor when you have completed it.

4. Never turn in any report, project, letter, assignment, etc., which you have not checked over and over again for accuracy. From your day of arrival, fashion an image of thoroughness and professionalism.

5. Take the time necessary to dress as a person in management should dress. From the very start, sell the idea that you take pride in your appearance.

6. Maintain a smile and a positive attitude.

7. No matter what may occur, don't destroy yourself by complaining, or slandering others. Bite your tongue if you have to. Chronic nay-sayers simply don't get promotions. Leaders find solutions.

8. If you know something is not right, and you feel like criticizing, don't. It will serve you no purpose. Figure out an alternative that will effect a positive change, then present it. And, do so, void of the tendency to prove someone else wrong.

9. Never argue. Nobody ever wins an argument. Does this mean you shouldn't disagree? Of course not. If you have a mind of your own, you definitely will have different opinions. When that time comes, however, stay calm. Don't raise your voice. Instead, bet a lunch or a cup of coffee. You'll prove you have management potential.

10. Look for opportunities to revise procedures, forms, methods, designs etc., that if accomplished, will save the company time or money. Many times it is just accepting as a challenge what everybody else is complaining about.

11. Make a point of taking notes when conversing with management or when in meetings. You'll be noticed for doing so. Also keep a daily log of your accomplishments. If questioned on a particular point, you'll be able to state how, what when and where. It is wise, too, to maintain the practice of making a "Things I Must Do Today" list every morning.

12. Have a good word for everyone, ... every day.

Information as to wages, job duration, employee satisfaction, fringe benefits, names of individuals who actually play a role in hiring decisions, and who at the company can be relied on to grant individual interviews should be maintained on computer.

When researching prospective employers, both teams and individuals should have access to these computer records and possibly to the phone numbers of former graduates who still work for the employers in question.

5. MAINTAIN AS THOROUGH AN ALUMNI RECORD AS YOU CAN.

As noted previously, the image of any school is primarily the result of the success of your graduates. In addition to keeping comprehensive annually updated records, you might consider having a GRADUATE HONOR ROLL. This will help you get your alumni to respond to annual questionnaires. Once a year, perhaps at commencement exercises, you can announce those being honored.

On the following pages, there is a 4 page form used by one school who has managed to keep excellent records. Read it and take whatever questions you want to use in your school survey.

GRADUATE SURVEY ON PLACEMENT

Name (optional) _____ Sex_____ Age_____

Institution Attended _____ State_____

Major Course of Study _____

Date of Graduation *(Please specify month and year)* _____

1. How many interviews for employment did you have, following graduation, before you were hired?
   ☐ 1 ☐ 2 ☐ 3 ☐ 4 ☐ 5 ☐ 6 ☐ 7 ☐ 8 ☐ 9 ☐ 10 ☐ Over 10

2. What was the date you were hired for this first Job? *(Please specify month and year)* _____

3. Prior to being hired for this Job, did you research the employer so that you were sure this was a good place to go to work?
   ☐ YES ☐ NO ☐ I never even considered doing this.

4. Do you still work for this same employer? ☐ YES ☐ NO

5. If you answered this question *YES*, are all the aspects of your position as you understood them to be at the time you were hired? ☐ YES ☐ NO
   Comment _____

6. If you answered question 4 *NO*, how many different employers have you worked for since leaving school? _____

7. Since your graduation, how many weeks have you been unemployed while actively looking for employment? _____

8. Are you presently employed? ☐ YES ☐ NO

9. If unemployed, would you be interested in Placement Assistance?
   ☐ YES ☐ NO

10. If presently employed, are you happy with your job?
    ☐ YES ☐ NO ☐ I could take it or leave it.

11. Do you feel that the wage and benefits you now receive are fair and equitable, considering the contribution you make to your employer?
    YES ☐ NO Comment _____

12. Would you leave this job if offered another at the same wage?
    ☐ YES ☐ NO Comment_____

13. As a result of your experience, do you feel you would now find out considerably more about the job and the employer before agreeing to change employment? ☐ YES ☐ NO Comment _____

14. At the time you left school, did you feel you were adequately prepared for the emotional and physical challenge of finding a job? ☐ YES ☐ NO
    Comment _____

15. To your knowledge, were classes, seminars or workshops available to those nearing graduation to assist them to develop their *"Job Search"* skills?
    ☐ YES ☐ NO ☐ I don't know.

16. Please describe any action you took to prepare yourself for your *"Job Search"* _____

_____

17. In retrospect, and in reality, were your prepared? ☐ YES ☐ NO
    Comment _____

18. In the course of your search for the right job, did you ever experience any strong emotional feelings? *(If so, please check the boxes below which apply)*
    ☐ Fear ☐ Anger at others ☐ Anger with yourself ☐ Frustration
    ☐ Confusion ☐ Loss of self-esteem ☐ Loss of self-confidence
    ☐ Despair ☐ Strong inclination to procrastinate ☐ Thoughts of suicide
    ☐ Other *(Please describe)* _____

_____

19. If you could relive your last year in school, and knew there was a course being offered that covered all aspects of the *"Job Search,"* would you attend? ☐ YES ☐ NO Comment _____

_____

20. Knowing what you know now, would you recommend that *"Job Search"* classes be offered in every school? *(Please check the box which corresponds with your feelings.)*
    ☐ YES, and courses such as this should be required to graduate.
    ☐ YES, but attendance should not be required.
    ☐ NO, for students should pursue this knowledge on their own initiative.

21. At the time you agreed to go to work for your first employer after graduation, did you get anything in writing in regard to your duties, pay, benefits, advancement, etc.? ☐ YES ☐ NO Comments _____

_____

22. When starting your job search, did you have a specific wage in mind that you intended to ask for? ☐ YES ☐ NO If *YES*, please state here what that wage was in annual salary. $_____

23. When interviewing, did you actually ask for this wage? ☐ YES ☐ NO
    Comment _____

24. When you accepted employment for the first time following graduation, what was the annual salary you started at? $_____
    Comment _____

25. In retrospect, do you now believe you could have gained a higher starting wage, had you been more thoroughly prepared for your *"Job Search?"*
    ☐ YES ☐ NO Comment_____

26. After going on job interviews, did you follow-up promptly by sending letters to each person who interviewed you? ☐ YES ☐ NO ☐ I never thought about doing this.

27. If rejected for a job, were you told the reason you were not accepted?
    ☐ YES ☐ NO

28. If rejected for a job, did you ask why you were not accepted? ☐ YES ☐ NO

29. If you answered *YES* to either question 27 or 28, or both, what response were you given? _____

30. Before starting your *"Job Search"* were you aware of the questions which legally cannot be asked? ☐ YES ☐ NO

31. In the course of any interview you have had, have you ever been asked questions which you now know to be illegal? ☐ YES ☐ NO
If *YES*, do you feel you were adequately prepared to handle yourself?
☐ YES ☐ NO

32. Prior to accepting employment, have you ever asked for either a job description or an Employment Contract? ☐ YES ☐ NO ☐ I never thought about doing this.

33. In regard to how you found the employer for whom you first accepted employment please check the appropriate box below.
☐ School Placement Depart-   ☐ State Employment Services
   ment Referral   ☐ Federal Employment Services
☐ Newspaper Want Ads   ☐ Private Employment Agency
☐ Random Mailing of Resumes ☐ Referred by a Friend or
   and Cover Letters   Acquaintance
☐ Yellow Pages   ☐ Other_____

34. During your job search, did you send out resumes and cover letters?
☐ YES ☐ NO

35. To the best of your recollection, how many resumes and cover letters did you send out? _____. Of these, how many companies invited you to be interviewed? _____.

36. Prior to mailing your resumes and cover letters, had you determined through research that these employers could better serve your desires?
☐ YES ☐ NO

37. Did you have your resume typeset? ☐ YES ☐ NO

38. Thinking back to the interviews you were asked to participate in, what do you think played a greater role in creating interest in your services,
☐ The resume ☐ The cover letter

39. When you finally accepted your first job after graduation, was it in the field for which you had been preparing? ☐ YES ☐ NO ☐ Somewhat

40. Since going to work, have you felt you made the right career choice?
☐ YES ☐ NO ☐ I'm still wondering

41. Knowing what you now know, could school personnel have helped you to be considerably better informed prior to making your decision?
☐ YES ☐ NO ☐ Maybe, but I probably wouldn't have listened anyway.

42. From your own experience, what would you advise students to concentrate on prior to starting their job search? *(Grade each of the following topics by circling a number from 1 to 10, with 10 being considered most important.)*

A) Knowing how to build self-esteem 1 2 3 4 5 6 7 8 9 10

B) Knowing, through self-analysis, the attributes you possess which will be of interest to any prospective employer 1 2 3 4 5 6 7 8 9 10

C) Knowing how to organize your time, set goals, and put plans down on paper 1 2 3 4 5 6 7 8 9 10

D) Knowing how to set up daily *"Things To Do"* lists ..1 2 3 4 5 6 7 8 9 10

E) Knowing how to locate employers who have the most to offer 1 2 3 4 5 6 7 8 9 10

F) Knowing how to research employers, prior to any interviews, to make sure you want to work there ...1 2 3 4 5 6 7 8 9 10

G) Knowing how to write a better cover letter..........1 2 3 4 5 6 7 8 9 10

H) Knowing how to prepare a better resume...........1 2 3 4 5 6 7 8 9 10

I) Knowing how to use the telephone effectively to follow-up and get the interview 1 2 3 4 5 6 7 8 9 10

J) Knowing how to look and dress your best..........1 2 3 4 5 6 7 8 9 10

K) Knowing how to talk, when to talk, and when to listen 1 2 3 4 5 6 7 8 9 10

L) Knowing how to respond to illegal questions 1 2 3 4 5 6 7 8 9 10

M) Knowing what statements to make to dispel the common concerns that every employer has....1 2 3 4 5 6 7 8 9 10

N) Knowing what statements to make in the interview which will set you apart from your competition 1 2 3 4 5 6 7 8 9 10

O) Knowing what questions you should ask in the interview to enhance your chances of being hired 1 2 3 4 5 6 7 8 9 10

P) Knowing how to prepare yourself to answer any question with self-confidence 1 2 3 4 5 6 7 8 9 10

Q) Knowing how to follow-up after the interview to improve your chances of being hired 1 2 3 4 5 6 7 8 9 10

R) Knowing how to get an employment contract so that the conditions of your employment hold true as time passes 1 2 3 4 5 6 7 8 9 10

S) Knowing how to conduct yourself from your first day on the job, so that advancements in both pay and position will be assured..............1 2 3 4 5 6 7 8 9 10

23. Please note here any comments, suggestions, or opinions you have relevant to this subject, which might prove to be useful in preparing graduates for the task of finding their *"Ideal Job."* _____

_____

_____

_____

_____

_____

CHAPTER 11

WHO IS A TEACHER?

One who provides knowledge, insight. By Webster's definition we all at one time in our lives are teachers. But the profession of teaching should be a far more exclusive club.

First, let it be clear that no diploma, no degree, no hiring contract so determines who should claim this title. The designation of "teacher" certainly cannot be earned as the result of scholarly preparation, as millions of learned men and women are incapable of passing on what they have come to know.

When students have been taught and are prepared to act on that knowledge, ... is it then that a person can say with pride, "I am a teacher"? ... No not yet.

It is easy to teach those who have come to listen, come to learn, so let us not so easily convey the title yet.

Earning this title must be reserved for those who can take each pupil before them, exclusive of none, and wholeheartedly give so all are touched, and influenced, and encouraged, and motivated, and feel that they are somebody.

It is the hug at the door when leaving, the tears on student cheeks, the memories lasting over years, the faith expressed which provided hope, the persistent "you can do it", the stern look in caring eyes, the goodness and the morality and the sense of responsibility which was evident by example, ... this is the stuff which gains this privileged rank!

So be more than an educator who teaches a subject. Be one who passes on how one might better live, avoiding those things which bring pain, ... providing foresight with all those things which can bring joy, accomplishment, and responsible co-existence.

Plan to be the one who a former student refers to as they stand on the highest step of the Olympic platform, or are interviewed after an inauguration.

When you hear those words, "I wouldn't be here today if it were not for ....", then it is you who can take a bow and take pride in being referred to as a teacher.

For only when all your ex-students say you are a teacher are you a teacher.

So from this day on accept this challenge: Choose no favorites who come before you and yet make all your students feel sure you have, ... and it is them.

INDEX

ABOUT THE AUTHOR

Richard Diggs is widely recognized for his contributions to the vocational sector of American education. A product of Detroit's parochial system and the University of Detroit, he has worked in numerous diverse positions which have included being a stock broker, banker, night club comedian, magazine editor, and free lance writer.

In addition, Diggs has owned twelve very distinct corporations including an advertising agency, a manufacturing company, three retail operations, a business consulting firm, and two schools.

Since 1965 Diggs has devoted almost all his time to some aspect of post-secondary education. He was twice elected President of The Michigan Association of Private Schools, was elected President of The Michigan Association of Vocational Education Associations, served as a member of The Advisory Council on Adult & Continuing Education for the State of Michigan, served on The Governor's Commission of Higher Education in Michigan, and founded The Michigan Organization of Private Vocational Schools.

Mr. Diggs served as a commissioner on a national accrediting commission for six years, 1972 through 1978, was active with The Anti-Trust & Monopoly subcommittee in Washington for several years, and was Education Officer for the Region 5 Executive Committee of HEW in Chicago under Dr. Mousilite.

After authoring the book, *Keeping Students From Dropping Out, etc.* in 1978, Diggs spent years on the road giving seminars on this subject throughout the United States. 15 other books followed, mostly on the science of getting a job. These included *The Great Job Hunt*, *Employability Plus*, and *Finding Your Ideal Job*.

Despite writing many books on "getting a job", however, it wasn't until he ran a degree granting College in San Bernardino, California, that Diggs concluded that the strongest factor we can use to retain students is assisting them to establish both career and employment objectives.

Diggs believes that an equal access to a better system of education is not only the solution to our problems, but the greatest contribution we can make to future generations